Satori Unwrapped

M000291167

Gerald "Satori" Seals II

Empowering Life International

Signature Series: Wisdom & Vibe Brand by Gerald "Satori" Seals

Satori Unwrapped

Published by: Gerald "Satori" Seals II, dba Wisdom & Vibe Brand, LLC

ISBN: 978-0692249260

Edited by: Anita "Amala" Jones

Photography by: JAdams Photography

Copyright © 2014 by Gerald Seals II

If we embrace our own story and remember our journey we can touch others. If we love and forgive enough we can advance ourselves and others.
— Gerald "Satori" Seals

Table of Contents

Satori Unwrapped...

Satori Unwrapped...

Satori Unwrapped...

Satori Unwrapped...

Dedication

In sincerity, I'm in personal gratitude unto the Most High. It's through your Divine Spirit that consistently gives me divine guidance, wisdom, knowledge, and understanding that enables me to help others as well as myself.

Therefore, I shall continually pursue a selfless journey.

To my children: Gerald, Shalom, and Jalissa, your generation shares the responsibility of bringing society back into the ways of love.

I also dedicate this book unto those that believe in communalism and unto the emerging and unborn generations.

~Satori

Special Thanks

To all those who've patronized the works and vision- the vision cannot be fulfilled without you.

To all the ministries, community groups, colleges and any assembly that has allowed me to share what is in my heart to their group-I thank you.

To the Personal Distributors, thank you for continuing to sell these works unto your family, friends and associates.

To all my brotha's and sista's who have been true friends, partners and a strength unto me, I truly thank all of you.

To all my virtual friends that have encouraged this work, I truly value you and am very appreciative of your support.

Love and Light!

'Satori'

Introduction

Life is about sharing our hearts. Within this expressive works, Gerald "Satori" Seals aka Satori, invites you on a poetic and expansive journey. This journey is what we call "Unwrapped," which highlights Satori being "open" through his poetry and life lessons. As you travel, you'll experience Satori's love, hope, hurts, transparency, inner confessions, desires, lessons, etc. Sensuality and sexuality are laced within these poetic expressions. Satori is often called a Love Poet and/or Wisdom Writer.

In the area of sensuality and sexuality, you can feel the freedom of Satori's soul. His poetry and writing style gives you permission to embrace your own sensual and sexual desires. Satori makes it ok to share pieces of your desires, thoughts, and hurts. This journey also invites you to celebrate love, romance, and intimacy. Even in the erotic innuendoes or fantasies, Satori shows beauty!

Behind each word or stanza is love. Virtual followers of Satori's poetry simply say, "We love it." There are times when you may shed a tear or tears because Satori truly introduces his heart as a man dedicated to loving and expressing himself. To be touched by this work is to receive a blessing." Take in the words, rhythm, and spirit of this work and let it massage your heart.

With many scenarios in life that we face, Satori's poetry and inspiration brings a peaceful confirmation to your soul. As you delve into this expressive works, you'll find Satori's poetry and lessons are socially, spiritually, relationally, and domestically relevant. We also invite you to glean deeper into the words and phrases and recognize concepts or principles that gives Satori's poetic works substance.

If we could describe this work in four words we would choose: **Confession**, **Beauty**, **Naked**, and **Life**. All these descriptive words revolve around Satori being "unwrapped" or "open". In **Confession**, Satori's poetry will reveal him admitting his desires and capturing his pain. In **Beauty**, you'll see Satori appreciating love, relationships, and being human. In **Naked**, you will see Satori being transparent about his feelings, sensual drives, and sexual desires. And **Life**, points to Satori being a Wisdom Teacher at heart who understands life--is a lesson. All of this is contained in one man. We applaud this work because we see Satori has embraced "unwrapping himself" as he continues his life quest.

Satori Unwrapped...

Confessions

Being able to acknowledge to ourselves our highs, lows, hurts, bliss, faults, desires and strength, empowers us to embrace and share our heart story. Confession isn't always spoken or written, it's also revealed in our silence.

Confession is giving ourselves permission to acknowledge what we already know what exists within ourselves. They say confession is good for the soul for freedom is near our confession. In practice, it's good to confess.

My Confessed Story

~Much love to those that can relate to this story

Here, lost in my room, ready to share this confessed story

Within the recesses of my mind existed a beautiful history

Today, I look at an old picture full of memories.

Strengthened to not throw it away even as tears confirm a short misery

I witnessed an unwarranted change in a beautiful story

Strong enough to face a past picture and was open to shed a tear

All I could see is a time full of love and absent of fear.

Everyone in heart was near

Innocence in my children eyes

Love protected us from lies

A heart became removed from love and brought about a demise

In an instant, you are now despised.

Hearts displaced and all I can see was a disguise

Laboring to build a name was now being defamed

Had to wrestle the shame

A heart removed from love created a period of difficulty

Personally never left love, therefore I had access to immunity.

Witnessed my children lives altered

Was hurt to see, at one time their hope withered.

A shift from love because of a conjecture!

Conjecture caused a change within my family structure.

My heart was shattered

My family vision became battered

I kissed my pain

I went through a period feeling socially stained

Stripped to nothing and all I had left, was love to gain.

Empowered to wrestle this dysfunctional drain

Love has enlightened me and I changed my name.

Love enables me to see this picture showing a beautiful memory

Love was once there but conjecture changed the story.

The absent of love changed my family

Yet, because of love I can rewrite my history

This man is nailed to a cross, and this is my confessed story.

I Miss

I miss how you highlighted my time

Remembering those many shared evenings

I was excited to just talk to you as we would recline

Each minute was a memory that seemed like a complete day

Remembering our anticipation as we enjoyed each other company while sipping Gamay

Remembering the scene at the reservoir as we sat by the bonfire making S'mores

With you was a celebration of simplicity as we both escaped complexity.

You understood the art of availability

You made yourself present even when you weren't available

I miss your availability

I didn't get a chance to tell you that I miss you

Jointly we were available and we shared that understanding.

Your sincerity was near to me

The simple text or call in the morning was dear to me

I love how you naturally spent time studying me. Let me just say Sexy!

You could explain my faults and weaknesses to me

If I haven't told you--that meant a lot to me.

I remember when you said you believed in my poetry

and even called me the modern day Rumi

That compliment captivated me.

You know exactly what to say to me. In case you didn't know--you are special to me.

Love is strengthened by understanding

Your understanding me, strengthens me

I love the fact when you weren't close you could project your love from afar

Just so you know that love was embraced.

Just know it shall rest within my heart and will not be erased.

You could see my heart behind my messages even inside my poetry

You even could hear my heart behind my oratory

I'm still amazed how you touched me from afar.

Our connection pushed the best in us as we raised the bar

I remember how we would listen to music as we rode in the car

I miss how you would tell me good night

You had a way that brought out my sensitivity

You encouraged me to keep my eyes on divinity

Your hugs and how you would rock me in person or in imagination were soothing.

To be honest, those moments were mesmerizing

I simply miss you.

I remember the light pecks even the ones on the neck

Those pecks were lovely as they were followed up with soft kisses

Such a feeling I can't miss

You helped me empty my heart so I could be filled with inspiration

I'm simply missing you--as I sit here in reflection.

Satori Unwrapped...

She Unraveled Me

She unraveled me emotionally

Her sincerity of heart penetrated me

Somehow she took my mind and made love to it

Her commanding draw made my thoughts submit

Her conversation opened up my mind

Her whispers removed any thoughts that could cause me to be blind

My mental is undone.

She gave oral loving to my imagination

That experience touched the recesses of my mind and just gave me that needed stimulation

She kissed my forehead and aroused my pineal until my mind became flooded with inspiration

She hasn't even touched me...but somehow entered me

I now realize she came in through the door.

Emotionally.

Satori Unwrapped...

Contemplating

Lost in emotion

Desiring a heart that can clothe me so I can avoid a self-induced suppression

Behind this veil of flesh, exists a heart that values emotional expression

Needing her heart so my cares can ooze like candle wax, so in time my healing hardens

Needing the presence of a woman's heart so my emotions can rest in her hearts' garden.

I'm a man that at times feels displaced in a foreign land

Shouldering the cares of my children, family, and friends while I fight the vices in the world

Can't escape these cares because I became my calling.

I'm a man whose innocence suffered false accusations.

A man that has witnessed others, along with myself, whose families have taken another course,

because of selfish motivations.

Yes, at times I cry about the broken foundations.

Once a man that was protecting his name while experiencing someone trying to bring it to shame

A man that has looked at family pictures to only to see his heart missing.

Striving to help many only to be attacked by someone that was dear to me

A man that has witnessed a life transition spearheaded by lies which sounded like a snake hissing.

Experienced division but fought for the sake of prevention

To be honest I crave a woman's consolation

At times the grief of wisdom suspends me, because with the spirit of wisdom-comes multiple revelations

Needing to unwind my emotions

I now seek a heart garden that carries my love potion

Strength I am, burdens I have carried

but there're times when I need a woman's heart to make love to me emotionally.

Satori Unwrapped...

I Choose You

I choose you

You agreed to share life with me

This day used to be a fantasy but saying "I do" made it a reality.

We are connected by light.

Each day with one another sends our hearts into flight

Together we soar above strife

As we fly, you and I realize that we are life.

We are of the same essence

In our alone moments we crave each other presence

This love is light as a feather

Knowledge, understanding, love, and forgiveness keep us together

Lovely walks

Daily talks

Random texts

Daydreaming about what's next

Encircled by love

Our hearts are molded into each other-fitted like a glove.

Baby, I'll hold the frame as you wear my name

We are walking intimacy.

Both found in this life journey

We unlock each other mystery

Our togetherness was found in our separateness

Love the idea of aging together but our love makes us feel ageless

Our kiss is timeless.

Security and Respect is an existing circle fueling our reciprocity

We celebrate each other's fragrance

Sounds of nightly rain causes our hearts to dance

We are sound

Our shared love is a melody

Every day with each other is history

You are me

Within you, I'm found

Our love is a venture-because we are partners.

Satori Unwrapped...

Travel with Me Emotionally

I remember you asked if you could enter my zone and travel with me emotionally

Gracefully I grabbed your hand and replied, certainly.

This touch and soft gaze is the beginning of our journey.

Without emotions we can't feel life

As you hold my hand and feel my peace transfer-realize

I am life

If you close your eyes you can see the real me

My true emotions are deep within me.

If you now open your eyes you'll see my emotions showcased in the land of living

Because you feel me now it's easy to sense me among the living.

Close your eyes

Touch me

Feel me

Grab me

Hold me

Relax until you are calm

Embrace my hand and feel the pulse in my palm.

Lean forward and allow our foreheads to touch.

You feel it--hold me tighter

This embrace is getting firmer

Both of our shoulders are clinched

Foreheads still touching

Our nostrils starts circulating our air rapidly

Our eyes are closed as we grab each other more tightly

Lost in our clinch

You feel me and I feel you.

Yes, we are traveling emotionally

Undefined tears begins to trickle

Tears drips slowly as your right cheek receives my wet sprinkle.

Slowly rolling our foreheads as more tears release

Here behind this peace resides pieces of my struggle.

This increased heart rate you feel are the obstacles I had to wrestle.

These feelings that sit under the light are my past dysfunctions that were touched by the light;

These inner scars near my heart are evidence of my fight;

Those images of water are my hidden tears that helped me overcome my fears;

These fragmented images are my disappointments that I faced;

The frequent images of me prostrate are glimpses of my daily prayers that have my heart laced;

The silence you feel and hear is my patience as I endured tribulations and overcame temptations.

These three lights near my heart is the hope I have for my children;

The scenes of me smiling is my inner joy as I witness my children's redemption.

This light you see shining within me is my divine vindication;

All these hues of light are energies generated from my meditation.

This openness you feel is my daily inner celebration.

These tears you now feel were my times of misery;

The peace and serenity you feel is the results from my transformation. The solace you feel as my tears hit your face is the joy I have from experiencing transparency.

Satori Unwrapped...

Random After 12 Thoughts

Lost in my after twelve thoughts, as I think of you

My emotions have no meaning-until it finds you

My purpose is absent of motivation-until I have you

What is the use of being the SUN and I don't have a MOON.

I need to give you my light...

My esteem is boosted as you receive my light.

I want you to know me

I want you to explore me

I want you to be open with me

I want you to have hope in me

I want you to love me

I don't want to run from being happy

I want to celebrate transparency

I desire to seek out new levels of intimacy

I desire to learn of your journey

I desire to combine energy

I'm wondering are you willing to change your frequency.

Would you go with me..?

Would you flow with me..?

If I accidentally hurt you, could you still celebrate me..?

Can we change the "I" to the "WE..?"

When I see YOU, can I see WE..?

When you see ME, can you see WE..?

Can we stand together in life and jointly see..?

Can we find joy in each other and just be..?

Can we invest into our history..?

Could we jointly own this journey?

Or, would you let go of me..?

Satori Unwrapped...

With My Inner Eye I See Her Heart

My inner eye took a picture of her heart

From the negatives the images of her light appears

I begin to see a heart of love and not a heart of fear.

I see her strength and sensitivity

She possesses a spiritual consciousness.

She knows how to fight selfishness with selflessness

She knows how to prevent the heart from becoming

restless.

Definitely a heart to caress.

She is apt to build consistently.

She practices charity

She is poetry.

I see vibrancy

Her heart contains positive energy.

Her company would invite you on a journey.

Her conversation is easy.

Her essence is full of grace.

With positivity she overcomes any negative space.

She is simply lights reflection.

She is skilled at yielding her heart under love subjection.

My inner eye beholds her.

I'm mesmerized by what I see in her.

Honestly I need her.

Her inner qualities creates this envisage of perfection.

Inwardly decorated and it shows within her projection.

I see a smooth soul...

A soul highlighted with a strong auric glow.

I see a walking symphony

I see her heart being free from envy

I see the embodiment of solitude

I see a heart not driven to be rude

I see mercy

I see quality

I see gaiety

I see harmony

I see her free from worry

I see intimacy

I see she can protect and further a legacy

My inner eye sees a walking prayer.

Her auric flare outshines all of her shameful past layers.

I guess what I'm seeing... is an appearance of my prayer.

Satori Unwrapped...

I'm Patient to Know You

Hey love, I stand in patience.

In my patience our differences are no longer a hindrance.

Tell me the meaning of your bodily expressions

whether it's aggressive or passive.

I'm patient, therefore, I can learn to know you.

Tell me the meaning behind your Ebonics, ghetto, educated or symbolic language.

I'm patient, therefore, I can learn to know you.

Let me learn your words, so I know how you organize your thoughts.

Knowing your thoughts, I'm equipped to massage and stimulate your mind while I advance your imagination.

I'm patient, therefore, I can learn to know you.

Talk to me about your life views & opinions, in that, I can connect with your perspective

I'm patient, therefore, I can learn to know you.

Tell me!

How you want me to touch you--whether it's for affirmation or stimulation.

Tell me!

How you want me to look at you, so I can talk to you with my eyes.

Tell me!

What turns you on so I can assist with your erotic desires?

Tell me!

How you want to be kissed, so nothing is missed

Tell me!

How you want me to move, so we can find our groove

Tell me, that I have permission to serve you

I'm here and I'm patiently waiting to know you.

Satori Unwrapped...

Why am I a Single Man?

The value of singlehood points to simplicity

Undress me until I am naked so I can begin again

I became naked as I face myself--laid out and bare

Open to see myself because love-of-self pushes me to care.

The value of single doesn't mean we can't relate; it means in simplicity we first relate...with self

Self was and self is...US

If we don't know "self" then we shall exhaust the "IS" and "US"

Why? Because the substance will be robbed from "US"

Singlehood is not a punishment, but a place for enlightenment

In my nakedness, I rebuilt my esteem.

I strive to reverse any energy that desires to lower my esteem

Reversal it is--as I forgive.

Evermore unfolded because I have the skill to forgive

Forgiveness brings me back to my singleness.

Affinity, unity, non-duality now exists within me.

My nakedness changes my attraction

Now single in heart because of the journey of transformation

Heart-mates attractions are quantum

My singlehood is energy

Relationships are to go from 1-to-2-to-1

Truly can't relate without singleness.

It's not about what someone can do for me

It's about the simplicity I can bring

It's the simplicity I bring to you and the simplicity you bring to me

People may ask: Why I am single?

My reply:

"I simply do not SEE...simplicity".

Satori Unwrapped...

My Love Puncture

I can admit I have a love-puncture.

Life continues and time waits for no one, but my heart is ready for this new juncture.

I've had enough time to lick my wounds

I can say that I have absorbed my love-wounds.

Self-healing has brought me to you

The moment I touched you, I knew what I have been missing!

Some holes need another to fill it in order to complete the healing

Your touched filled the holes in my soul

No more energy seeping out!!

No more light seeping out!!

I can say I'm no longer leaking,

As I'm able to hold you I feel pure containment!

Addicted to the moment

Your touch brings a new enlightenment

Your touch is erasing the memories of my fragments.

Geeesh, your forehead resting under my chin brings restoration

Your kiss takes my shame and makes me honor my name

Been alone and I've tried to live for myself and I struggled with it

My sense of completion comes when I'm serving you and others,

because I'm a man that have to be mindful of others.

Keep touching my heart.

I'm becoming sensitive.

There was a time of raging waters in my life.

Your touch calms my waters

Scoop me with your hand and see how soft and nourishing I can be--because I am calm.

So past all weariness.

My running waters will extend life so we can grow,

Taste the waters of my heart because it's full and absent of holes

You filled me!

Now we can create our happiness.

Satori Unwrapped...

Feeling Some Kind of Way

Just feeling some kind of way...

Many emotional roads I've travelled and I'm weary from carrying the load

Getting past my pride, I admit a woman's presence is a desirable abode

Roaming alone, but I'm attracted to an open heart.

Very burdensome when I can't take my feelings, thoughts, and emotions and just unload.

My heart yearns for something higher,

Heart is reaching fully extended

There are times when I've felt like life has ended!

Life is in sharing hearts and that experience is priceless,

To interact with a closed heart is lifeless.

Such a reality is an aimless pursuit

I can't hide in a closed heart when ultimately my heart craves life.

I want a glass of water with some jazz playing while you rub my head added with good conversation

Just having someone to greet you brings a sense of relaxation.

Oh, I know what this feeling is...

My heart yearns to be touched.

Satori Unwrapped...

Your Waters

You help me see what is inside me

Your love for me is like clear waters

Despite our flaws, your love is pure.

I have no choice when I see you to also see me

You projected a love upon me that made my heart respond to you.

You saw the love in me and you demanded it out of me!

Your clear waters has awaken the love that exists inside me

This awakening caused me to love you

How? Because as I love myself...I see you

It's from my inner exploration that has caused me to see.

Many seek and search for their love interest outside themselves versus being met by the love existing inside.

Your love is the inner lamp that have illuminated the dark rooms within my heart.

Your waters refreshes therefore our love becomes our liquid solace

The softness of the exchanged waters softens our flaws

Sipping each other waters and from here our love will pour like waterfalls.

Satori Unwrapped...

I'm Captured!

It is cool to be captured!

Within my inner most being I desire to rest in your "lap of life"

while my head is being stroked by your intoxicating finger tips.

Interpersonally exchanging our breath

Simply just enjoying us.

Letting the mystery of our energy speak!

Allowing our hearts to be in tune to each other's language.

Searching for each other's music is only heard behind the breath as we relax each other.

A joint gaze reveals so much!

As I look into your eyes, I find my inner sanctuary

Let me rest.....I'm captured.

Satori Unwrapped...

Brougham Ready to Change the Scenery

Brougham is out canvassing the scene...

Open to love and ready to be with a Queen.

He has spent countless hours, days, and years expanding his heart capacity

Enlarged enough to fit his queen within his heart cavity.

His stride is still graceful

His demeanor is still peaceful

He is not afraid to be sensual

He loves the sexual!

Deep within...his inner eye is open

His sight surpasses the selection of feminine tokens,

He is looking for a lady well spoken.

Brougham is looking for a woman that invests into her inner decorations,

He is looking to see if she can or will endure life tribulations.

He is looking for that lady that knows how to recline

Brougham eyes are open to that lady that invests into polishing her mind!

Not looking for a student....but a woman that is prudent

He needs that woman that is witty and sexy,

Not witty to match wit but a way to meet each other's knowledge intimacy.

A woman that is comfortable in her sexy,

A woman that knows how to honor secrecy,

Brougham is searching for this because he has spent time with himself intimately.

His love of self, heightens his love frequency

His vibe is still grown and sexy

At times you may say he is grown and sultry

Most importantly, his vibe is easy

Brougham isn't unfair in his expectancy

He is balanced by becoming the lessons while pushing himself mentally

He desires that lady that brings some mental therapy.

Brougham is realizing it is crowded, so he is ready to change the scenery.

Satori Unwrapped...

My 12 O'clock Confession

Caught within my 12 o'clock confession

Engulfed within the silence of my mind desiring esoteric

lessons

Smoke pervading the air

Exhale as I release all cares

Open

Clear

Now ready for this 12 o'clock session.

Environment on ease as I sit engaged within my inner

exploration,

Dim lights and smoke sets the tone for my heart and

mind as I enter within this counseling session

Inhaling until my thoughts are near

Now ready to travel on many emotional levels

On one front I value singlehood because of the joys of

isolation;

Then on another front I crave connection

Just an honest confession.

I wrestle with desires of isolation & connection

Heart within this conflict hangs in a balance

because at its core it loves silence.

I find myself toggling, because I can find silence at both

ends of the fight.

There's silence within isolation

Silence is also found with having a connection.

I'm in touch with my sensuality...

I'm moved sexually...

To be honest, within this confession at times I prefer

isolation.

I crave isolation because it stimulates my thoughts and

assists my need for inspiration

Again, to be truthful I have a strong desire for

connection

I need intimate interaction!

I need that one-on-one communication

I need that touch that sends me into reflection

I need to connect with a heart of consolation

I need that kiss that dismisses my tensions

I need those kind words that heightens my elevation

I need that random head rub that sends me into

meditation;

Just honest confessions.

I suppose I have a strong desire for connection

I want uninterrupted romantic feelings

I want a relationship full of meaning

I need someone that seeks understanding.

I need her to be open and not into vain demanding

I only say this because I believe in a connection that is

ever flowing.

Smoke still clouds the air...

This confession has released my thoughts into the air.

Truly, this is a therapy session

I thank my heart and mind for this 12 o'clock confession.

Satori Unwrapped...

Can I Escape In You?

Just wondering if I could escape in your arms?

Being held close feels like hearing a violin string being stroke softly;

Your warmth chisels my ice and invites us to share in our confidentiality.

Our secrets are kept between us and sacredness relaxes us from being alarmed.

Currently in my feelings and needing help to explore what I am sensing.

The softness of your bosom balances my emotional dualism

Remembering how your hands caressed my head as you held me closely

Pinned on your chest, you whisper: "Let it go"

The presence of your whisper, silenced my emotions

I realize the answer I need is within your whisper as you repeat: "Let....it....go!"

Your embrace defines why I am within my feelings

The need of human touch has me in my fullness and I desire to fill your emptiness!

My emotions are silenced because your embrace is my garden;

Your embrace is the seed that arouses my heart and prevents it from becoming darkened.

Your caress makes my heart hearken.

Your hands has a way of listening

Your hug is my therapy!

I'm able to release my feelings, because you have a unique way of listening.

Today, I need you because I need to unload this fullness.

I feel your therapy because you bring me emptiness.

As you touch me, you draw my fullness until it fills your emptiness.

In your reception you become strengthened because you gave me emptiness.

This unique draw is a mystery.

A draw not easily ignored because we share such a strong chemistry.

Satori Unwrapped...

In Your Presence

I'm refreshed by your presence

I love bathing in your essence

Your energy is like a lit candle

The light of you is as a beautiful fragrance

Within our interaction there's no dominance

Just pure romance.

Soft horns play as our hearts dance...

Call this a lover's groove!

Enjoying each other without anything to prove

This tango has our hearts within a trance

The pressures of the day fading as our hearts finds its' place

Our intention is interwoven within love.

Time together are moments of exchanging love

The reflection in your eyes are pure as a dove

Your energy makes me want to fly

Your presence ignites my heart

Ascendancy with you is an ultimate high

You unravel mysteries and answers my questions about the WHY...

Your heart is a love sanctuary

Your words are poetry

Interaction expands our love capacity

The glow from your eyes creates an ethereal canopy.

Comfortable with you because love is your company

Our time together is pure harmony!

Absence of rigidity but your presence refreshes me

You are like a taste of water

Your love will not let my heart falter.

Nothing pressing...

Time together is just

Refreshing!

Satori Unwrapped...

Digging You

I dig you

U-m-m-m-m-m, I sense something

I feel something

I'm heightened by my intuition.

Why am I pierced with this subtle heart-felt elevation?

My heart arise, my soul is alive, my mind is clear and it's indifferent from fear.

My motive and intention feel genuine

There's something compelling me to be refined.

Somehow, I feel an inner soothing!

My heart is being massaged

I'm so moved by this conclusion...let me shut my eyes.

Um, let me resonate and harmonize upon this envisage

I'm moved by your presence!

You don't even need to speak because your presence speaks volumes

This explains why in this envisage I am so consumed.

Hold up!!! I know this presence, I have seen this presence.

It is the missing "me" that will complete me

I sigh....I pause....I still my mind....I control my breath

I see me in you and I see you in me!

So far...yet so close, but our hearts are drawn near.

Isn't this something: I don't even know your name!

Your presence encourages me to overcome my shame.

Your presence is the "ME" that I can't get out of "ME"

It can only come from you.

So I guess you are the one that completes my milieu!!

Your presence sends waves of serenity and tranquility

You possess a quietness and have a finesse that's stronger than shallowness.

Grace put us in this place and I can finally see your face!

Satori Unwrapped...

Will You Fly Away..?

If I provided a cage and left the cage open would you fly away?

Inside this cage is a productive economy

This cage contains plans for us to produce something domestically

This cage is an environment that'll ease you psychologically

This cage contains a vibe that will activate you spiritually

This cage hosts a strength in my male energy, which will balance you emotionally.

Here, in this cage we can converse telepathically.

In this cage there's no limits on how I'll serve you sexually

This cage is filled with intimacy!

The atmosphere in this cage heightens our affinity

Wondering if you'll stay with me?

Like every bird, you have the right to fly

The cage door is open....I just wonder if you will choose to stay with me.

Like every bird, you can choose to leave the cage and fly without me,

Hence, if it is love you won't think about escaping me.

Our love is within this cage with the cage doors remaining open

This love is a "choice" to live

Our intimacy is for us to enjoy!

Yet the question remains open....will you fly away or stay?

Satori Unwrapped...

I'm Thirsty

Walking alone can be exhausting.

Needing that feminine energy that quenches my

masculine thirst

Desiring a nice...long.....drink

Desiring an open atmosphere where we can just think.

A thirst that causes our hearts to seek each other

company

I need your company!

Your energy alone is plenty

Someone to pause with as we share our epiphany

Desiring a true connection that is refreshing

An open flow that is not limited by us asking

My heart requests to connect with someone

who celebrates me and not invested into hurting me.

Craving that connection that makes loving easy,

Needing that unforced desire to share intimacy.

You have no problem telling me that you need a drink.

That feeling moves me to pour you a glass.

Our hearts openly communicate that we are thirsty

That strong resonation makes finding US...easy!

Craving that loving huntress of Light

This draws me...so your light gives me sight.

Both of us connected--not separated

Wanting that feeling knowing that we are the Sun &

Moon paired

Sharing our thirst boosts our emotional highs

Being connected spiritually, so we can share our karmic

ties

Wanting that thirst that leads to a love affair

Lost within each other so there's nothing to compare.

Both of us being thirsty gives us enjoyment in security

Both of us loving the simplistic and are quite domestic

Needing that moon that controls the tides of my earth

Needing that feminine grace quietly affecting all life

As we share our drink we flush out strife

Having the mindset of preferring to just share ONE

glass

This reminds us that we prefer to live in each other

Both of us desiring our company to be secluded instead

of sharing it with others

This thirst means we can work together

One moment you are the nurturer

Another moment I'm the encourager

Our thirst causes us to value the domestic

Needing that lady that will say, "Instead of two glasses

let's share one"

It's in our share that keeps our life simplistic.

Satori Unwrapped...

Your Voice

Your voice....

Your octaves used to sooth my soul

Your voice use to enliven my heart

Now I hear silence

Absence

Empty space, ready to capture and reflect sound.

A different need

Simply craving your voice!

Your words, ideas, and tone used to stroke and cleanse the windows in my heart

I am looking out the windows of my heart open to hear that sound...YOUR VOICE!

Subconsciously, I desire to respond but there is no voice.

Your voice used to send me into a moment!

The melody in your voice caused me to dance

Your voice used to bring hope!

There was no voyage that seemed impossible.

I miss the small things that have so much value, such as your voice

Imagine life without a voice

Love is a sound and the voice transports love into hearts.

Life without voices stagnates hearts.

My heart desires to be touched by your voice.

Without your voice I am hindered from exploring my heart.

I desire to draw from it but my heart is missing you.

I can't hear the harmony in the airwaves because I am missing your voice.

Satori Unwrapped...

Confession of a Single Man

This day I realized I was bringing picked roses to my past relationships.

A picked flower will soon die because it was removed from its life source.

As I stand as a single man I realized I have picked too many roses

Suffering from the matrix indoctrinations has altered my reality of a true relational perception.

Gender harmonizing has become a lost skill

Why? Because I have picked too many roses

This day I unlearn the picked roses' belief.

I shall now bring things with a pleasant scent

This day I shall take my next relationship to a rose garden.

In my confession....I desire to bring life.

My Love Affair with the Pen & Paper

Think I'll spend the night with "pen and paper" tonight

She has a way of capturing my thoughts

She's the type of lady that invites a brainstorming session

Personally, I love it because those are the best intimate moments

I like how she shares her words and captures expressions

She always has some type of creative flow that she is open to receive

She takes me

She receives me

She recites me

She captures me

I like the dual vibe she gives me

On one side she is straight and right to the point

Then on the other side she has a way of being flexible and allows room for me to make mistakes

I look forward to the music, candles, and a charged creative atmosphere

Looking forward to sleeping with my baby...

Pen and Paper!

Satori Unwrapped...

The Fathers Silent Cry

Fathers, the Most High hears your silent cry

The struggle to fight to sustain your name.

You have fought and continue to fight through the web of insults and seek for light as you silently cry

You remained silent when others tried to desecrate your name

Still, you silently cry.

Your attempts to be there were waived by her desire to hurt you

As any man, you tried to fight and went to court and got hit with child support.

No one sees the social impact you now face.

Striving to live and had to move in with family and friends just for self-support.

Still, you silently cry.

You used to hear your child's cry but now you are silent as you listened to the emotional-based lies

Some forget these lies make you silently cry.

You have interest in your child but you are tired because you know the emotional fight doesn't stand in court.

Money depleted, so now you're not available because of self-support.

As a man, you still fight even when hope is out of sight.

You gather yourself and strengthen your shoulders so you can reclaim your name

In your cry you realize your unmentioned shame can be a support to boost your game

As you reclaim your name, your child's eye will recognize fame

Your child's measure of fame is to know that you love them.

You have to fight through domestic obstacles... just to prove that you love your child!

Fathers---the Most High sees your pain and be assured the Spirit shall assist you as you rebuild your name!

Satori Unwrapped...

Beauty

Beauty is evident to those that see beauty within themselves. Beauty still

exists and is seen and felt as we embrace our flaws. Celebrating the

human

experience is to not dismiss the unpleasant but to embrace them. We

can't know beauty until we know the ugly. Beauty is not measured in

looks but according to how we impress each other. To say something is

beautiful is to admit to what has impressed us.

Satori Unwrapped...

Silent Wonders

A night filled with silent wonders

Mysteries of hearts has drawn the love of whom I ponder

A nice venture to learn about each other sacred features

Raptured by your unspoken

Caught and lost in my imagination

This mystery is making the thought of you fonder

Waves of possible ideas have my desires suspended in time

The wonder of you is blowing my mind!

In this imaginative place there's no limitations or desires that come to mind

Desiring to see what drives you.

On this night, I'm curious about what satisfies you?

On this night, I want to see your inner potential

Your mystery is electrifying and mesmerizing

This mystery of you overwhelms me

because tonight... I just want to learn and know you.

Satori Unwrapped...

Shadow Dancing

Sitting here, I just took a voyage in my imagination

In this imaginative sphere I have this fixation of this lady

Glad to meet her!

We now exist in this realm of ether

Today, I'm "shadow dancing" within my mind!

Dazzled at how your energy is swirling your femininity

Sensually analyzing one another's qualities.

Hand extended...

Life transfers from my palm and our energy is calm

Softly pulling you closer, within forearm length.

Both of us sensually swaying

Lost in each other energy.

My heat encompasses your body

Movements speaking

The beat shifts

So does our energy

Joint-intentions are being felt

Our embrace became serious

Body and heart making this moment a memory

Still in my imagination, I desire to convert this moment into a reality.

All of these visuals going on inside of my mind.

Still holding you...

I feel your energy pulsating around the small of your back

No doubt this energy is stimulating.

This shadow dance is breath taking

We're just stepping and our pace is slow

Too bad this is just my imagination, because I love this flow!

Satori Unwrapped...

The Day of the Brougham'

It's cool for the young lads to rock sneakers. There's a point when a man graduates past a trend and embraces his style. Embraces his flow with grace as he tips his hat at the young brotha's stuck in a trend.

Chivalry is no longer a choice but a state of being......and this is his delivery.

Easy flow is his motto as he adjusts his tie and adjust his pants legs so he can show his flats. He's moving past relaxing in the Pubs for social interaction. This brougham' relaxes at the grown sexy lounges or parle' at a wine loft sipping a glass of Vino. He may entertain puffing the latest Cuban cigar as he plays with his cufflinks. In tune with the times, he may read the periodicals in Barnes & Nobles to stay current.

He desires to be well-versed in the schemes of life so he can shift with the times. Not BOUGIE but sees the need for re-positioning. A man discovering his "love of self" enables him to help others build value themselves. This brougham' secretly desires a partner and is shifting his vibe so he can change his status. His maturity and coming of age arouses his mind to realize he is needed to keep his community sound.

Observing the young lads walking, he realizes they're absent of a visual forecast on where to transition too. This brougham' realizes he must insert himself amongst the young lads, so they understand the mark of a distinguished gentlemen. Seeing young lads rocking tees and skinny jeans but absent of sight for the next level--which is style!

Style is inner expression and not imitation. Polished, well-read, knowledge of life, socially conscious, holder of perspective, and ready to be accountable on behalf of his lady and family. Call this brougham' an example of a cross-over. A collision of trend and style packaged in one. There are many sides to this brougham'.

He realizes he must be seen in the community so the young lads can aspire for maturity and a social graduation. This brougham' draws a distinction in these young lads minds. The young lads locked in a trend are looking for combat, attached to their momma, strive to intimidate, and defines himself by possessions. Contrarily, the brougham' is good at all skills but a master of none: handy, intellectually resourceful and quick, a great communicator, artistic, a magnate, strategic, unifying, and a reconciler of the young lads.

This brougham' is needed to spark the young lads to become aware of the trades, encouraged into exercising their intellect, guided into polishing their souls, skilled in home management, domestically competent, and just BEING masculine poetry. The day of the Brougham' is here ladies, we are rising and coming. We may have exchanged suit for steel-toe boots; but know, we are the Broughams' and we are coming to uplift our young lads. Time for a resurgence of MASCULINE POETRY!

Satori Unwrapped...

Friday Snow Night

Friday night snow layered from afar

A snow night to be in the company of somebody that cares

Someone to kiss and someone whose heart you can share

Wrapped tight within the blankets

Shared glass of vino

Piano keys in the background being played by Dino

Sipping by the fireplace while we enjoy each other's space

Wine glass reflecting the flames and the smiles on our faces

Pecks and kisses as the snow covers the deck

Playing sensual games around each other's neck

Anticipation is jointly felt

Even while it is cold we cause each other's hearts to melt

Lovely evening while we sit back and watch the big screen

All we want is each other's company.... because our time is serene.

Satori Unwrapped...

This Type of Love

Our love contains no shadows

Our reciprocity of love prevents our hearts from being shallow

Call this a LoveBow

Current times of love waxing cold makes us a rarity

Our love for each other is serenity.

Our interaction is pure tranquility.

Your pureness causes me to experience a satori.

Your love invites an inner discovery

Loving you is a practice of charity

You invite me into my intuitive enlightenment

Every day is filled with excitement.

We realize this love is immeasurable

The closest way to measure is to say this love is pleasurable

This love surpasses the humanistic and invites the cosmic.

My eyes are burning

This experience is electrifying

You are hypnotizing

You have my soul pulsating

Every day now becomes exhilarating

Our holistic fit is breath taking

Addicting

Mesmerizing

Tantalizing

Soothing

Enlightening

Rejuvenating

The very essence of us is restoring

With this type of love there's no pretending!

Satori Unwrapped...

This Love Is Fiyah!!

Beyond obvious colors

We're entangled within heat fusion

Can't put this Fiyah' out until our fiyah is done burning

There's no end to this flame because this flame is

flaming.

Energy

Combustible synergy

Both feeding off each other's energy

This flame is untamed

Who can quench this fusion?

Polar entanglement

Our heat is as close to our cold

Like gold, our passion burns in each other's love-mold.

Locked by heat

Open to each other's heat

Yearning to receive your heat

Consumed in each other heat

Call us Fiyah!!!!

Our corporal is burned until our love is no longer

temporal.

This fiyah' causes our heart to beat.

Heart pumping flames

Melting into each other names

Enclosed into the elemental

Teased by each other subliminal

Tempted by our sexual

Drawn by the mysterious continual

Take my fiyah' and I receive your fiyah'

It's hot!

Radiation of love is how we greet.

In heat we meet

No need for water

Our flames can't falter.

This love is Fiyah'

Satori Unwrapped...

A Shared Glass of Vino

A glass of vino shared with you would be alright

Desiring to taste something bursting with floral & citrus aromas

Craving a semi-sweet wine that's slightly sparkling

Rich taste of peach and honey on my palate would be a delight!

A nice bottle of D'Asti would be soothing.

To be honest it's easier to enjoy the single life if I had somebody to escape with

Plenty of time on hand.

Plenty of interests come to mind

Would love to exchange thoughts & ideas with a woman that uses her mind

Just desiring some good company.

All about helping each other unwind

Easy vibe mixed with some laughing

Letting moments and time speak while sipping.

Music playing with each note changing the atmosphere.

Convo allows us to penetrate each other thoughts

Lost in each other's company makes it appear that time has been caught

Finding ourselves in each other's comfort is time well spent

Suspended in the moment because we can just recline and enjoy this glass of wine.

Lady Grace

They call her lady Grace

A woman whose essence exceeds her pretty face.

A true lady

Not shady

Confident in herself as she defines her own pace.

Yes, you can call her Grace.

Not in competition because she knows her place.

No need to compete

Everything within her is complete

Her originality is unique.

Her style is chic (sleek)

She commands her presence!

All you can do is recognize her essence.

Her energy sounds like a piano

Her sway has a natural flow

She makes herself of no reputation

She is the epitome of self-education

She carries lessons.

Entertaining her is an invitation to self-exploration.

With her there's only elevation

She is like a dividend paying stock.

She possesses a valuable mind that can't get blocked.

A woman of wisdom...

A woman with insight that can build kingdoms

She is music...

You can feel her acoustic

She captures moods

Her intention is for the good

Yes, lady Grace.

A promoter

A facilitator

A motivator

An innovator

An incubator

A partner

A supporter

A builder

A leader

A woman that jump starts the heart like a defibrillator

She is sound

Her words are profound

She is a living decor

Someone a man can adore.

Satori Unwrapped...

You Are a Hidden Gift

As I lay to rest

I thank the divine for sending me someone that I can lay it all to rest

The treasure within I hope to produce the treasure for us

Trials in life have a way to teach you how valuable it is to have a woman to love you...a precious gift.

My heart is becoming consumed in the mysteries of you.

We both desire to give a piece of ourselves that hasn't been given to others

That sharing is what will keep us sacred.

To take my name and to say it so heartfelt is a gift I never had

This type of a marriage I long for but it something sacred for you.

I love you and your presence is a gift to me

I can now truly love again... because you're a hidden gift that I'll will spend the rest of my days unwrapping.

When Love Is Present

When love is present....all things can be supported

When love is present....harmony is embraced

When love is present.....a relationship can be sustained

When love is present.....all fear dissipates

When love is present.....two can trust

When love is present....there is balance.

Satori Unwrapped...

She Grabbed My Pen

In the calm of the night within the midst of the early morning whispers

The soft flow of the night awakens me

Overshadowed with inspiration I go to grab my pen

Gently her hand covers my hand and says, "I can feel your inspiration."

She then says, "I will hold your pen and I will write from what I feel and sense from your heart"

She advises me to recline in thought and yield unto the high frequencies of love

As she embraces my pen she begins to feel my heart trajectory

Similar to a sonogram she picked up my vibrations and begin to write as she felt my frequency.

The lessons begin to translate onto paper as the pen shakes from my heart trajectory

She begins to click the pen while in repose as she yielded to my thoughts telepathically

As she received meta-thoughts her fingers adjusted as she was overloaded intuitively

Enraptured within the write she leans forwards and kisses my pen as the weight of my channeled passion rests on her back.

The reflection of the moon shines upon her as the light highlights the pens chrome which is adjacent to the deck

Adjusting the pen she uses the tip to massage her temple and also her neck

Her other hand touches the iPad as she selects a jazz song to channel

Melody and harmony fill the room as the soft trumpets blows.

Fully engaged she explores concepts and begin to decipher between case and argument

Fingers gripped more strongly as she strives to highlight lessons that leads to enlightenment.

Smiling she says, "I enjoy your morning energy"

Her eyes this morning revealed that she has studied me

Our history of love making allowed her presence to conceive my essence.

This morning she changed the game!

She picked up my pen and begin to channel me and became my name

This morning she used telekinesis as foreplay

Her holding my pen elevating our intimacy

She not only just feels me, sees me, hears me....but now she channels me!

My Eve of the morning grabbed my hand and became officially my pen.

This morning I'm assured we'll write each other legacy

Each word written is connected with our intimacy!

Satori Unwrapped...

Remembering the Time We Spent

Thinking about the time we spent

The grace of her touch heightens my senses as if the wind blew her fragrance.

A nice calming experience.

Our interaction is a social massage

Our chemistry is a symphony

Her conversation draws my words from the depths of me

Our togetherness was raised out our separateness

We are most together when we are unaware of our togetherness.

So natural that we are pass mental or preferential calculations

Together we have access to pure moments.

Time shared draws out our vulnerability to the point that we both can share and just lament

We wear each other well, which strengthens our time spent.

Our kiss is the rain

Moments being wet reduces our pain

Completely penetrated by possibilities

Within both our hearts we understand each other completely

Because we are both open, we experience chemistry that flows freely

Every time we talk we visit feelings hidden behind our minds

Our togetherness arouses our minds to remember our shared time

We even share unconventionality

We both desire to move past normality

Both of us are mesmerized by each other's mentality.

Can't forget our experience.

Random moments throughout the day filled with surprise hugs.

Ending the day on a nice rainy harmonic night as the back door was open

while we lie upon the rug...

Remembering the time we spent.

Satori Unwrapped...

In Appreciation

Your purity radiates through your eyes and sparks my calm

Interesting because time spent with you is as a living psalm

Differences we have but we have a strong connection

Your grace brings my attention to love and that is perfection

Your heart to me is a healing balm

To be with you is consolation.

Now that I spend more time with you I'm starting to miss your calm vibration

Your simplicity meets the depths of me

Moments are celebrated with time and more time increases my appreciation

Life alone can feel so random

Having you opens my eyes sparking hope to live life with you in tandem

I know everything happens in due time but drawing close to you I anticipate becoming one

Unknown journeys are possible if we enjoy optimism.

I Can Hear You

I can hear the light in your soul

Your sound resonates!

Your sound liberates!

Your sound elevates!

Your sound vibrates!

Your sound stimulates!

Your sound penetrates!

You and I are rhythm!

I hear you and you hear me!

Together we are just sound!

Satori Unwrapped...

What Makes You Smile..?

Queen, your smile moves me

I must admit, I desire to know what makes you smile?

The comfort and warmth I feel behind it makes it clear that you are not juvenile.

Your smile engages me

Curious as of now, are you smiling at me? If so, what do you see?

King, I see your heart reflecting the origin of the universe, the cosmos

It's that reflection that causes my lips to separate in joy, laughter, and a faint smile

Queen, your smile sends my soul on a galactic journey

Your check bones are radiant as the moon at night

That glimpse of reflection pierces the depths of me

Your cosmic glow is a draw that invites the universe to be the author of our shared verse

Your smile is music...it is eclectic!

The white gleam from your teeth is artistic

Your smile is poetry

Queen, your smile sends me

The joy I see is as if you are painting upon my heart like an artist that paints on a clear canvass.

King, I would be remised not to acknowledge the boldness of your strength

The length of your legs delights my imagination to the places they've carried you and places they've seen you through.

Your hands resemble the hands of a god crafted with integrity and passion

I long for words to drip from your lips to nurture my soul.

Saturate me

Your presence captivates my breath and hold it in abeyance

My heart pants and longs for your love

Let the journey unfold to sacred territories of pleasures

Queen, territories of pleasure are a worthy voyage as I would love to search your hidden treasure

Many places I have walked in my journey I have surveyed life

As you smile I see your light

Satori Unwrapped...

As your lips arches and as your dimples show--your passion can become my guiding light

This abeyance is strong because the adjustment of your smile shows the prism of your heart radiance

I can drip...I can pour...I can touch

I can walk within your imagination and find solace within your passion.

King, Love..!! My imagination is curious and is limitless.

Are you ready..? You are the object of my search

I study your breath... your smell...your sounds...your visions....I consume you.

I see the longing in your heart.

I will patiently do my work

No worries, no rush I will continue to sew my passion into your heart and design a tapestry of love never encountered.

For the moment just rest in me.

I will replenish you from weariness.

I was designed to carefully adorn your body and mind with my love and lust

To touch you in places that sincerity aches for my only touch

Shhh....come close. I have a song only my body can sing to you.

I won't interrupt. Do you hear the melody..?

Queen, I not only hear you, but I feel you!

Residing here is where we are meant to be

Our souls are limitless... your touch has my soul in flight

As I fly...hold my string as I rise like a kite.

As my soul flies I realize there is a rise in your heart and I'm pursuing what is within sight

Rejuvenation is here...Elevation is here....Hope is here....Harmony is here...Love is here

I love this place behind your smile.

I now know what makes you smile

You smile accordingly to wherever your heart is near.

So, as we both now stand our hearts are here

I see your smile, so I know your heart is near.

Satori Unwrapped...

Brotha's, Tell the Ladies: "We see it!"

You needed to share your emotion

My hug gave you a rejuvenation

We kissed and it made you cry

Not a cry of sorrow but a cry of release

You felt my sincerity so your emotions were unleashed

As a woman and parent you've been shouldering burdens and needed a relief

Children crying

Washing clothes

Paying bills

Cleaning

Homework

Working

All makes life at times to feel emotionally draining

Hidden frustrations leads you to question what you are gaining

The workload of life makes you feel isolated

At times you desire that touch so you can feel connected

Not in dire need but just wanting a human touch so you can feel naked.

At times you look at your past decisions in disbelief

In those moments it brings about temporary grief

As kids rest in bed you spend time questioning your beliefs

You refrain from sharing your feelings about this

All because you feel that no woman should feel like this!

All these feelings were pinned up until we had this kiss

You wonder at times if a man can sense your inner toil

The answer is...Yes we can!

This moment my kiss was like soil

Instead of you pumping life....my kiss gave you growth and life.

My kiss allowed you to be affected by my sensitivity.

You cried because you have permission to share your vulnerability.

Satori Unwrapped...

Just Being

Out of our gushing streams reflects the ecstasy that we have found in each other

This stream is unlocked because of the enjoining inside one another

This flow is a sign that transcends us past time to just "BEING"

I AM....SO I BE!

YOU ARE SO....YOU ARE!

Both of our streams are warm like a hot sauna

I desire you and you desire me, so we are what is to "BE"

Be in the moment!

BE with me!

BE love!

BE ME and let ME, BE you!

We exchange BEINGS so we just BE what we need from each other.

Nothing complex....just BEING!

We are invited into a new height that is before us as we strive to "BE"

A level where love is "US" and it no longer have to be received or given because we are just LIVING.

This might be heaven I feel inside you.

Why? Because heaven is just BEING!

If it is heaven all we have to do is just BE

Simply....Love

No longer have to prove it because love has become what we shall "BE"

and that......is LOVE.

Satori Unwrapped...

Life with No Limits

Love knows no limit!

Mysteries, unfold

Our intense gaze is told

Breathing your air and near your heartbeat

Our eyes are closed but there's still an envisage

Simple touching noses transmit messages

Sending shock waves of transformation in our total being.

Call it butterflies

We are still breathing

If I....If I.... If I... would touch you it would confirm light between you and me

Anticipating oneness.

Breathless.....yet we are still breathing

Our life is breath, therefore you and I breathe.

Inhale and exhale for out of our breathe life flows

Today, I breathe your air because I want our life to have no limits.

Satori Unwrapped...

Limitless Love

So much to explore in this thing we call love

Love is kind...Love is patient... Love is beauty... Love is tolerant

Love is forgiveness... Love is energy...Love is life...Love is hope

Love is timeless...Love is limitless

Love is like flowing water, refreshing whatever it touches

Similar to the river flowing into the ocean

As water, love is essential to supply life.

Just as curiosity questions the depths of the ocean that encourages many to entertain

that inner search within the abyss of our heart,

That's how love is making you want to search more and strive to explore.

This search within our heart asks, "Do you want more?"

This exploration, vibratory intoxication, mystifying journey,

exhilarating experience...opens the depths of our hearts

Gushing, flowing, and oscillating

as the waves of water speaking within our hearts.

Open it is, willing to make room for your heart.

Willing to greet your heart ...willing to touch your heart,

willing to protect your heart...and willing to love your heart

Love, has no limits!!!

So, why stop here?

Why settle here?

As we love ourselves, so we shall search ourselves.

We welcome this task of searching the limitless love that dwells within our hearts

Can we go there?

Let's dive into each other divinity and excavate our serenity.

Let s search each other hearts so we can draw from our cisterns of limitless love.

Satori Unwrapped...

We Are Dancing

We are dancing and gliding in this moment of mystery

We are close and I'm not far from your ear

Your heart is open.

I whisper and the drum in your ear sends a new rhythm and beat to your heart

Can you hear me baby?

Whispering in your ear as we move,

Hearts are getting locked and there's no interference to disturb this groove.

The softness of my whisper sends electromagnetic signals to all your touch points

This energy will not stop at your meridian points.

Our touch is sending biological alarms to all of our touch points

You feel me baby?

The very heat from my breath touches your ear and sends a tingle around your shoulders and relaxes the base of your

neck. Rocking slowly as we gaze into each other's eyes

I allow my index finger to slowly touch the base of your neck

Pulling you a little closer, I simultaneously let my fingers slowly move from your neck to your shoulders.

The fingers on my other hand move from the small of your back, crawling slowly towards your shoulders.

Both hands are parallel now softly holding you.

I take advantage of my height and pull you closer to my chest.

Paused....while our eyes are closed.

Anticipating my touch...still swaying to the music...I kiss your forehead

Thoughts generated and the possible mystery is racing

Your defenses unfold but you realize we are just dancing.

Satori Unwrapped...

Baby, Relax In Me

I'm so ready to escape the monotony of today

Ready to lay aside all the hats we wear throughout the day

Baby, you have to realize activities never cease

I've been longing for you because our togetherness will assist our needed release.

I know you need to feel vulnerable and free

Unwind and tell me what's on your mind?

You want sacredness, I can close the blinds

Secluded we are, tell me about today's battle scars

Be the river and empty yourself into the ocean of my heart.

Our unwinding opens our streams of intimacy

In seclusion our vulnerabilities becomes a ground for our serenity.

What felt so taxing....has now become relaxing

Fire place blazing

Tension is replaced with jovial play

Interaction is free as we listen to Sade'

Soothing feeling and we're both ready to dine.

Listening to "Cherish the Day" as we share a glass of wine

As you unwind...and relax in me.

Satori Unwrapped...

Unspoken Word

If I could tell you how I feel my words couldn't capture the unspoken

My feelings for you only can be translated into action

My hand is extended inviting you to a joint-experience.

You are designed to live

My desire is to pump life into you

Breathe Ma'.....I'm here

Our words are exchanged breath

You and I can give each other life

My unspoken words is the breath I desire to share with you

I never stop wanting to love

I never stop wanting to care

I never stop wanting to share

My passion overwhelms me and at times it's hard to bare.

Being able to be vulnerable again is a desire

Past hurts have caused me to be scared that my love will be thrown up in the air.

Interesting, my love was meant to be tossed because you saw value and snatched my love from the air

Life changes are meant because it hard to make love when nothing is there

There's a place in our love making where our souls are bare

I desire to be at that place so when we are done we can look at one another and simply stare

Within speaking a word.

Satori Unwrapped...

This Night

The easy breeze grazing the outline of our bodies

Stirred by the breeze arousal

Rainy nights like this make it appropriate to put water and air together

This fusion makes me crave your aquatic-harmonies

mixed with your soothing winds....grazing areas that need attention

A night prone to love

A night vulnerable to touch

A night for spontaneity

A night for caressing

A night for expression

Tonight is a moment to admit that: "I love you"

Tonight, rain on me and blow your winds on me

Just as air and water shares oxygen

I desire to share my oxygen with you.

This

night

Satori Unwrapped...

She Was Hiding Inside Me

Knowing love resides within me but where can I go to exchange it?

I wrestle in the ring, Me versus Compatibility.

I also wrestle with Me versus Personality.

One thing I know, when Love is present I will SURRENDER.

Therefore, pin me!

My heart desires to lock with another heart

but I wonder where can I find it?

Do I have to travel?

Do I have to network?

Do I have go to a party?

Do I have to meet her through a friend of a friend?

Where????

I hear my inner voice continually say..."It is in you"

What is in me?

LOVE is in me and I crave to exchange it.

Is it you?

Is it you? I guess I will give up!!

Hold on, as soon as I gave up somehow I found her.

Nothing fancy but she is true to herself.

True beauty because she harmonizes with her soul

Her heart is being rebuilt with the bricks of loving herself

How in the midst of a sea of people am I attracted to her?

Again I hear the inner voice say..."It is in you".

I looked into her eyes and I was softly pierced by the energy from her heart.

Instantly moved....again, I hear that inner voice say... "It is in you!"

My attention is "frozen" in the delta of her heart

Suddenly, I'm moved to surrender

She speaks plainly but she spoke to my heart.

DANG is this her?

Now we both stand holding each other attention.

I hear again.... "It is in you"

We kiss!

We dance!

We talk!

We cry!

We cook for each other!

We complement each other!

Now we F-E-L-T each other!

Now I feel at home because my heart has exchanged love.

I found her because I saw her IN ME.

My heart was able to lock with her heart according to the love that I have within me.

I guess this is why I found her....

because she was hiding inside me!

Satori Unwrapped...

I Surrender

It is nice and healthy to be able to extend your heart with someone you have special interest with

Being in someone's presence that loves and values you increases your energy field.

Having someone to enjoy and exchange intimate life moments with is a necessity for the heart

Entangled by trust, hope, love, forgiveness, communication, self-discovery and intimacy, locks treasures between two

Being with someone that believes in love empowers two to create one environment that generates life.

Experiencing the bio-rhythms merging into one heart beat is a joint-venture worth investing into.

Love...is worth the investment!

The return is intangible and life sustaining

Exploring the love within your soul and inner most being is a voyage that is detoxifying you from low-energy fields

Having regular, sensual human touch brings the sublime to an apex

In my vulnerability, my soul finds home in true intimacy and love.

Vulnerable I am. My soul and heart are at rest.

In my vulnerability, I'm not ashamed to love and be loved

I surrender.

Let Our Hearts Become Naked

Daily obligations and routines in life can cause US
to lose sight or desensitize US
from knowing the hearts of those close to US.

Sometimes we have to push the pause button so we can serve, see, and hear the heart of others.

The heart may have a cry, concern, ambition, hurt, shame, disappointment, hope, vision, or fear but we have to allow
moments
for our hearts to speak.

We have people that are close to us but are we sensitive to hear their hearts?

The issues of life flows from the heart

If we can't see, hear, feel, or touch one another's hearts...our issues will continue to flow

If there is an issue in a relationship, create time and space so there is an opportunity to see each other hearts clearly

Let our hearts become naked so the issues can stop flowing!

Satori Unwrapped...

I Haven't Even Touched You

Your self-love is blowing through my soul

Ummm, your very presence is like the calming spring breeze grazing the soft side of my skin.

You haven't touched me but your inner projections feels like an Asian massage

I'm feeling all of these emotions inside and I haven't even touched you.

The power of your intention is like a tonic that is relaxing as the scent of lavender

Still mesmerized because....I still haven't touched you

Your calmness is tantalizing my senses

Your scent is aromatherapy to my soul

Heightening my sensuality because of the positivity behind your smile

Your love of self, activates me astrally

Perceiving your aura suspends my senses

Causing my soul to travel....Here I am

Amazed...because I still haven't touched you!

Feeling a certain way about you and I haven't touched you

BUT

YOU

TOUCHED

ME!

How can we be present but absent of physical touch?

I guess we just experienced a meta-physical touch!

Satori Unwrapped...

Just One of Those Nights

Just one of those nights where we define our own moments

Easy vibe, glass of wine, and nice movie while we sit by the fire

Nothing demanding just some grown snuggly type stuff

Enjoying each other energy

Paying attention to the mystery of each other's soul

Tasting the wine off of each other's lips

Quiet, hmmm....real quiet, if only we could read each other thoughts

O-N-L-Y if we could read each other's thoughts!

Maybe there's nothing to read because we currently have no thoughts

We are just in the moment.

The mystery of our souls is being spoken through the subtleness of the night

Interesting and thoughtless

Nothing to think about when there are no rules of engagement

This night is just open and full of mystery.

Our mysteries are found in our openness

Yes, it is obvious this night is geared to sensual moments

Here there exists no barriers...just different levels of touch

Vibe still nice!

Wine is still right!

The Shiraz is taking effect now...we are highly attune to each other energy while we ignore the movie.

Why watch something that's already defined

when there exist no thought because we now occupy each other's mind?

Just one of those nights

No apology needed when we are highly prone to be GROWN.

Grown enough to act out our own movie

Grown enough to express our sensuality

Grown enough to practice our own physical pantomime

Grown enough to practice, joint-yoga

Grown enough to create our own mysterious sound

Even after the resounding sensual activities we both in our exhaustion can define our silence.

Truly, it is just one of those nights.

Satori Unwrapped...

My Heavenly

You are my heavenly experience.

That feeling of peace, closeness, acceptance, feeling wanted,

continual bliss, being jovial, and the overflow

of inner silence.

Being with you is like climbing a cosmic ladder.

Your touch, hugs, and kisses doesn't have to

lead to eroticism.

You open doors to my sense of security, serenity,

psychological intimacy, and an enthusiasm for life

So Heavenly!

No doubt, this is what makes you my heavenly experience

It is the reciprocity of feeling you have brought me to

I can escape!!

It is now easy to survey my life landscape.

As the air blows, as the water flows, and as the sun pierces the sky

I just love to look into your eyes.

For inside...I see life, hope, calmness, support,

Drive to love, openness to forgive, and an openness to receive love.

It is you heavenly presence that lets me escape and causes me to embrace love.

I feel covered, please don't turn your heavenly off or I'll feel uncovered.

I desire you, think often of you, and imagine things about you.

All of this in addition to your affection and intimacy!!

What else could there be?

I appeal to you to always show your affection and intimacy

because this makes my life

heavenly.

Satori Unwrapped...

The Kiss

The softness of our lips freezes our whole anatomy

One kiss can connect us for a lifetime.

Yeah, I still remember it

Frozen in my mind....THE KISS!

Our kiss connects life

Our kiss connects emotions

Our kiss enlivens

Our kiss suspends time

Our kiss explains what we can't say in words

There exists an inner odyssey that can only be unlocked by our kiss.

Our kiss is the gateway for our souls to travel

In an astral world with no limits and boundaries

Light is generated!!

Our hearts are penetrated!!

Comfortable being above life's entanglements

while enjoying being connected to our intellectual,

emotional, and sensual union.

Our passion, interests, desires, hope, and anticipation are shot through our whole being.

Ummm, our kiss is ecstasy!!

We give each other a rise.

So elevated simply by, THE KISS!!

Kiss me!

Absent of THE KISS exposes our

co-dependency to have that KISS.

Kiss me!

I'm so addicted to our kiss.

I wonder why???

Why, because THE KISS creates bonds

And we are forever bonded by....

THE KISS

Satori Unwrapped...

Can I Have A Moment With You?

Can I explore you..?

Can I talk to you..?

Wondering if I can have a moment with you..?

As a matter of fact...I may need two!

I want to listen to you

I'm open to your words caressing me

No need to be bashful...I can keep the mood light and playful

I'm concerned with you being comfortable

Easy conversation

Jovial atmosphere encourages our connection

Laughter is equivalent to libation

Time together is pure relativism

The silence after the laugh is pure escapism

A day of putting our expectations away

Sense of freedom....even when it's time to go we want to stay

A moment to say: we are present

Lost within our company is like receiving light from the moons crescent

Our guards are let down...Loving our privacy

Joint understanding as we learn each other's history

A time to relax our shoulders

A time to share laughter

Joint-ease encourages us past our shames

Both are real and are above the games

We can care less about past names

Loving the mentioned

Loving and listening to the unmentioned

Comfort of conversation encourages innuendos

Feelings are crescendo

The joy of the moment has my heart speaking in a falsetto

A day to celebrate transparency

Time spent reminds us it's ok to be happy.

Satori Unwrapped...

You Pull the Romance Out of Me

Baby, you don't have to say a word because you pull the romance out of me

A romance motivated by a true desire to bring us closer.

I already see you....this romance doesn't need to be requested

Why, because I'm emotionally and sensually invested

You just think and feel it and I'll catch it

You'll know because my acts will show it

This romance you pull out of me causes me to tell you things I didn't know existed within myself.

Your romance is a light that allows me to see the love within myself

This romance is about taking your Love-of-Self and my Love-of-Self to rise to a level of abstract beauty

Why go out for dinner when I can feed you..?

Why go to a movie when we can write our own script..?

Why hold your thoughts to yourself when you can just share it with me?

Why listen to your girlfriends love stories when this romance is calling you?

This romance is an escape from one world to another

Leap into a world where the definition is painted by our feelings and passions

Yet this world only exists if we pull the romance out of each other!

Satori Unwrapped...

Our Love Secrecy

Got off work and came home to transparency

I opened the door and I'm greeted by the love in your eyes

Wonderful feeling because love met me and I felt your intimacy

Sincerity begins to cloud the atmosphere as we unwind

Open ended questions, so there always room to invite each other to understand what's on our minds.

As we exchange answers through conversation, we strengthen our secrecy

I know you and you know me...intimately.

Home atmosphere simply open because we are free from fear and ulterior motives,

Our egos are displaced, which brings our home into unity

Here, in this home you can cry, vent, fall short, say the wrong thing, and think the wrong thing

and you know it goes no further than the front door

Why, because we value our secrecy.

Baby, coming home to you makes my life clear to me

Our love is an occult and we are sworn into secrecy.

As I Awake

Truth is when I open my eyes in the morning, I desire to see you

Every blink is a snap shot that freezes your image in my mind.

I'm trying to live this life seeing you.

My eyes record each moment, so when you are not present I can recall your essence.

Beauty is said to be in the eye of the beholder.

Call me the beholder because I have taken enough blinks to only see your beauty

I only have sight because of light

Each time I open my eyes in the morning I see light.

A place of transparency

The sight of you is so dear to me

I see you and you see me

In many ways this is intimacy

It's intimate because every time I see you I get lost in the sight of you

I have awakened and see the truth:

Love is in the sight of you.

Satori Unwrapped...

She Just Is

She commands herself

She is self-empowerment

She projected a radiance and I was caught paying attention.

She seeks no reputation

She is truly a walking meditation

Her rhythm is reggae

Naturally being real is her forte'

Her treat was to add to my book collection

She appreciate ancient wisdom and she added something to the Vedic tradition

Interestingly she pointed to the Upanishad, which means sitting down near

Her unmixed vibe coupled with wisdom had me wanting to sit and hear

She spoke commentaries about life

She shows interest in lessons that make the soul rise

At times I was suspended especially when I looked into her eyes

How she read me was to my surprise

She has embraced Queendom

She is freedom!

She speaks wisdom!

Casually we walked through the book store

Inner thoughts were connecting and sending neurological signals saying, we want more!!!

Over dinner she spoke with gentleness

She said, where there is separateness two can find their greatness.

She continued to speak and said: one sees another, smells another, tastes another, speaks to another, hears another,

touches another, and thinks of another, in order to know one another.

A brotha had to pause and fumble over my thoughts as I saw another piece of my truth

Her swag says...send it on me

As I now lay in bed

Simply...envisioning.

Satori Unwrapped...

Mahogany Glow

Her soul is full of harmony.

She has a jazzy essence like she's from Philly.

Definitely a grown woman and nothing about her is

silly.

I like how she embraces me delicately.

She engaged me as she elevate my vibrations.

She strengthens my self-exploration.

I'm caught

I'm being taught

This energy can't be bought but must be sought.

She possesses a glow.

Her eye gaze matches her flow

If I could nickname her I would call her: Mahogany

Glow

Her physical contour invites my curiosity more.

She is the epitome of femininity.

Her heart is ruled by serenity

She controls my attraction

She shifts my frequency.

She etched herself in my memory.

She touches the back of my neck gently.

She blows in my ear softly

She tickled me with a feather erotically

The ice on my back melted rapidly

She used the melted ice to massage me.

Deep thing--she hasn't even touched me sexually!

Her focus was to penetrate me sensually

At times she'll kiss me gradually

and then switch to kissing me frequently

She has no problem initiating and touching me

creatively.

Did I say she is jazzy?

Did I say her vibe is like she is from Philly?

I was feeling her inside me without her sexually

penetrating me.

She's skilled at stroking me emotionally.

Her finger tips were shifting me neurologically

She still hasn't touched me sexually!

She continues to stroke me mentally

Candles burning as she kisses me gently

taking random pauses to recite poetry

As she whispers my skin increases its sensitivity

Both of us share a high frequency

She re-wired our codes telepathically

Call it neuropsychology!

She took time to connect with my personality.

Mahogany Glow spent time touching me sensually until

she touched the essence of me.

Satori Unwrapped...

This Morning She Fed Me

She awakened me this morning...

not with her natural scent

Nor with the scent of food

Nor was it the lotion that smells like spearmint

I was awaken by her silent prayers.

Her earnest petitions were on my behalf.

Prayer is two ways, so her conversation with God caused me to sense that she was divinely petitioning for me

I was awakened this morning by the petitions from her heart.

My eyes slowly open and she just pulls me closer

"Ahhhh, the scent of divinity"

Encased in her bosom I realized this is the garden of serenity.

She gently strokes my head as my energy points activate until I feel like jelly.

Holding each other as the soft sound of the Asian flute is playing.

She kisses my temple and then whispers: "Let's talk about the ancient sayings...."

I'm still mesmerized because I was awakened by her divinity.

Loving this morning because she saw my need not to feed me food

but to feed me divinity

and hide me within her

Serenity

Satori Unwrapped...

Let's Dance Baby

Feel like listening to some smooth,

Soft, sensual mood-based grooves

while kissing in the rain

To just be lost in the sounds as the rain touches the street,

rocks, the hood of the car, leaves, and as it pierces the softness of the wind

Baby, let's take it back to the days when we would dance to the vinyl records playing.

You become the record and I'll become the needle.

Let me touch you until your sound plays

Easy tune

Soulful groove

It's like this when I'm with you

The crackle gives us the authentic feel because we aren't perfect

Perfection is the quest as we dance in the sound

Luther

Freddy Jackson

Frankie Beverly

The Whispers

Anita Baker

El De 'Barge

Minnie

Isley' Brothers

Us.........just whispering to each other

Solid mood

Ole Skool music is purely our soul food

Let's dance Baby.

Satori Unwrapped...

She Touches Me Mentally

Our conversation is laced with mental poetry

Words laced with a sensual cadence

Psychic waves generates an ambience

My mental is recalling things from remembrance.

This is mental intimacy

A psycho-therapy

A mental refinement

Our mental exchanges are enlightenment

Our minds are open until liquefied

We open each other up until we can see what's inside

We are sharing a mental journey.

Comparable minds are hard to find

There's an art to this mental element

Telekinesis is a tool to help our discernment

We see through each other's motives and intentions

Our words are pure seduction

Our hearts strengthens our intuition

Sharing ideas births our inspiration

Her mind polishes me.

She penetrated me through inquiry

Our minds met and explored possibilities

Her mind is not scared to investigate.

We are two halves of each other

Our thoughts are seeds and soil of one another

Being of the same thought, cause our love to grow

together.

Our mental exchanges whisper for whisper.

Our mental exchanges desire for desire

She kissed my thoughts

She hugged my thoughts

She investigated my thoughts

She penetrated my thoughts

She entered my thoughts

She is me and I'm her, therefor we are thought.

Her thoughts stroke me innocently

We convened together

and unto each other we projected intimacy.

Satori Unwrapped...

We Be

For ME to SEE what WE BE

It is you that soothes me

Comfort I have with you because you embrace me.

You don't hide your feelings from me.

You take time to communicate with me.

You see hope in me.

You desire to grow with me.

You share knowledge that helps me to see.

You help me become selfless so....I can see.

We entertain the same lessons so we can jointly see.

You pose questions that lead me to see.

We value each other therefore....I see.

You keep me balanced therefore....I see.

With you there's no judgment, criticism, or excessive emotions, therefore....I see.

We are open to each other and that causes me to see.

We are love and forgiveness and that helps me to see.

You see me and I see you so....We Be.

We share transparency therefore....We Be.

We seek each other's interests therefore...We Be.

We hold each other's attention therefore...We Be.

We enjoy each other therefore...We Be.

We are not worried about others' opinions therefore...We Be.

Our aim is to serve each other therefore...We Be.

Patience is exchanged with us therefore...We Be.

We endeavor to cover each other weaknesses therefore...We Be.

We accept each other mistakes therefore...We Be.

We secure each other therefore...We Be.

We love each other therefore...We Be.

We bring peace to each other therefore...

We Be.

Satori Unwrapped...

Cosmic Love Call

A true cosmic love call that activates my love draw

Magnetism radiating from your soul

Connection is the demand

A true demand asking for a supply of my selfless soul to

touch your true essence

A true call to beauty

A beautiful soul sounding its' song

Who can hear?

Who is near?

Who can bear?

Who truly cares?

Your heart is magnetizing love to be in the air

You are drawing my soul because it's bare

Us together is intimate alchemy

Pour out and pour into me

Search me!

Satisfy me!

Lift me!

Please me!

My magnetism is strong so, you can escape in me

No need to question intimacy

My ego is gone, I just want love to dominate me

Your love reverberates!

Your intention penetrates!

Your words stimulate!

Your kiss captivates!

Your touch activates!

I'm lost within your gaze

The light in your eyes open your maze.

Your eyes of understanding is water to my soul

Refreshed by your cisterns

With you love is a desire to learn

Water me!

Refresh me!

Take me!

In our clinch we exchange essence

As we exchange we become ONE in presence.

Satori Unwrapped...

Just Me and You

Such an easy and mellow night

Listening to sensual music, eating fruit, and inhaling the fresh scent of a mango-peach candle

Just me and you in each other's sight

We can call tonight:

Just Me & You

Sipping wine and talking about lessons that are divine

Escaping all complexity

Our vibe highlights simplicity

Just another great moment with you

Open conversation is our preventive measure to avoid future apprehensions

My words are dancing in your ear

Teeth clinching your ear lobe s-o-f-t-l-y as I whisper:

MOMENTS

This night is so open when I hear you speak I can hear the meaning under your words.

This unspoken dialogue is saying: COME CLOSER

I reply to your unspoken request and ask: COME WHERE?

Your unspoken reply...COME CLOSER TO MY HEART.

Anticipating this beautiful moment because tonight I'm going to make love to your heart

Our hearts gyrate with the rhythms of our words, ideas, feelings, emotions, and intelligence.

The effect: our joint-orgasm will be our spoken word

All we can say,

Just

Me

&

You!!

Satori Unwrapped...

I'm Pressed to Love

I'm pressed to love you

You are simple and absent of riddles

You just desire a man that desires to be settled

I match that desire.

As a matter of fact, I want my love for you to inspire

Seventy-two subtracted from forty-one gives us a gap of thirty-one

Too much time in-between, I refuse to be blinded by unending fun

From your mouth you said: You are done

Again I desire the same—as a matter of fact, we can create our own fun.

Your heart is inclined to build.

I desire to bring to you my love and skill.

Not driven to cancel your ideas but I desire for our ideas to combine

Both of us are tired of fantasy

We have no tolerance for flattery

We each want to say....Someone loves me!

We are desirous to explore the infinity of love's mystery

Truly, I can say love is the re-birth of a new me

You refresh me!

Your love washes me!

You motivate me to cover you!

I'm not scared to care for you!

I have no problem to admit that I cherish you

You are my treasure

Yes, you agree to also be my pleasure

My heart is open, so you can paint your picture.

Let my love be your rapture

I'm yours for your pleasure

To be honest I can see in your eyes that love is evermore.

Satori Unwrapped...

Close the Door

The doors of my heart are available to you.

Come in and decorate

fumigate my inner chambers with your fragrance

Do this unto us in remembrance.

Love can't be a hindrance

Put up a beautiful picture that will prevent our love from being absent

Polish me so I can improve my temperament

Make this place in my heart a pure enjoyment

Bring in the new furniture so it can fit my heart's contour

Greet me by saying: "Bonjour"

If you enter in alone

you are all I need...so close the door.

Can We Create a Beautiful Love Song?

If love is a sound then we should "be"

complementary vibrations that produce that sound.

How can someone desire love if they don't resonate that vibration?

If the aim is the sound of love then our vibration must be of that sound.

Man: Do I resonate a love vibration?

Woman: Do I resonate a love vibration?

Man & Woman: If we come together what will be our sound?

Life is rhythm

Harmony is unity

Sound creates music!

Can we come together and create a beautiful love song?

Satori Unwrapped...

Joined Together

I'm in love with the melody of your soul

You move my bio-rhythm

Similar to an inspirational hymnal

Your melody is subliminal

I respond to you without knowing

Engaged within your sound and our love is growing

Call us a garden.

Our hearts are ripe for pruning

This process gives us meaning

The end result--our hearts towards each other are beaming.

Not only one--but both of us are submitting!

United unto the divine source which influences us

This is the source that checks us.

This is the source that sustains us.

This source is the glue that ties us.

We are simply yielded to divinity.

In light--we be.

Our yielding dismisses ambiguity

All we see in each other is clarity

No place for duality because we love our unity.

Our love is easy!

We found the secret in our simplicity.

We embraced our togetherness metaphysically.

Call it a graduation from a soul mate to a heart mate or twin flame

We were in love before we knew each other's names

We're now joined together and love is our aim.

Satori Unwrapped...

Our Visual Story

Here there's no doubt

We tried but we prefer together to take the scenic route.

Life obstacles

Emotional debacles

Moments of tests and trials

Tribulations

Assaults of humiliation

Disappointments

Unemployment

Through it all we learn to be each other enjoyment.

Through it all you always touched my heart and said:

"WE can face this..!"

Our love language is absent of the word called, dismiss.

20 years of love that never left, even though at one time

we went down a different road.

Our love is constant and in US was a love that became

our abode.

In US exists a sacredness that is untold

In the midst of shame you still held onto my name

Love is our gaze

We have mastered how to overcome life's haze

The test of time truly has proven that our hearts are still

ablaze.

We are family.

We love each other's company

In support of each other we started our own company

We are sharing history!

We are being history!

Our children have a legacy!

This love touch is bliss

Each time we touch each other it becomes like a kiss

Our faith used our trials to create our patience.

Love is patient.

This is what we have because we are each other's other

half.

We became a fence to each other heart even when it was

dark.

We had our time to fight duality but now we live in

unity

Today, we understand that we are each other's family.

We are an episode unto each other and the only take is

for us to BE

Today we are a picture in memory

that is telling a visual story.

Satori Unwrapped...

Naked

Nakedness is to be uncovered and not be ashamed of our own feelings, sexual drives, sensual needs, desires, thoughts, or aspirations.

Many shall label theses degrees of expressions as explicit. Explicit is being comfortable with sharing and expressing what others feel should be ignored or hidden. Nakedness is an inner discovery to know ourselves more intimately. Exploring our personality, emotions, spiritual nature, mindset, motives, intentions, sensual nature, and sexual energy encourages us to embrace our nakedness. In my nakedness I am personality! In my nakedness I am spirituality! In my nakedness I am volitional! In my nakedness I am sexual!

Satori Unwrapped...

The Scene within My Mind

You are the highlight within my mind

Your vivid images are a mental concoction

Visuals are so intense my mind is throbbing

Think I'm suffering from a visual intoxication.

The movements and moments are prolific

Each highlighted image is specific.

Your search is very inviting

I see a lot of pecking

I vividly see a lot of biting

I also see a lot of touching

Breaks and intermissions for random massaging

All I want....is you!

Your sensual and sexual command is so demanding

The nature in me is moved to be in a place of serving

So intense....you started running.

You weren't running too fast,

you just needed a break from cumming!

Ummm, loving the capture

Locked within your legs

Subdued by our sensation puts me in a daze

Panting rapidly and slowly as our breath is confused

because we are trapped within a sexual craze.

This visual is so clear the moon can be seen during the

day.

Full moon giving us permission to play

Now laced with your taste

Pulsating and clinching

Needing a moment from our bodies flinching

Taking another intermission for some rubbing

Calming our muscles while we are both sweating

Drinking water to prevent us from fainting

Tongue softly gliding upon your lips

Continuing to flow until my lick touches your hips

The shakes oozes liquids

We now share in our liquid solace

Both listening to our acoustic sounds

The sound is thick.

Dimly we stare while appreciating the sound.

Now erotically moved to reward you with another lick

Position switch!

Both in a position where we both can kiss each other tips

Patiently serving each other as we take time in this place

Gentle blows cause us both to flow

Cuddling

Sharing

Kissing with a new taste similar to nectar

Just resting upon each other

We end in a relaxed state

Silently wondering....when is our date?

Satori Unwrapped...

I Want to...

The desire within my heart needs to touch you

Countless alone evenings

No one to touch causes an inward teasing

Heck, this stored energy is an emotional and sexual treason.

Craving your touch

Needing your touch

Endless thoughts alone are just too much!

Forget my ego, I need my heart and whole being stroked

Honestly, I need to serve you...

I want to massage you...

I want to touch your energy and perform Reiki on you...

I want to blow on you...

I want my hands to gently caress you...

I want my knuckles to knead you...

I want to take my time with you...

I want to bite you...

I want to lick you...

I want to circulate the energy inside you...

I want to make music with you...

Can you feel me..?

Can you hear me..?

I want to take an erotic journey with you.

I want to drink you...

Be honest I want to taste you...

All this is in my heart.

Truly desiring a counterpart

Needing someone who can share in this energy

Someone that understands no rules--just pure ecstasy!

Someone who wants me to move them sensually

Someone who wants me to move them erotically

Someone who wants me to touch them delicately

Someone who wants to share a lifetime of intimacy

Yes, into you I see

Yes, into you I want my permanent residency!

Satori Unwrapped...

Shared Intent

Her teeth clinched my lower ear

Holding my ear lobe she whispers.

Immediately–I felt her wish.

Slightly adjusts my neck and shoulders thinking how I can meet her wish.

Open to hear the message behind her words

Intently listening, so every word is heard

So much behind this whisper

Her soothing tone makes the possible prone

She speaks and my heart becomes prostrate

Such a lovely whisper.

Our closeness makes her sound crisper

She whispers again--now I can hear clearly.

She said: Good Morning (with intent)

I replied: Good Morning to you!

From there we shared our intentions.

Kissing the Wine off Your Lips

Kissing the wine off your lips

Mesmerized by the suspended time

Your kiss is sublime

My palate stimulated by the wine's texture

Rolling the wine within my mouth until it softens and soothes my tongue

Such a nice kiss!

Soothing to my senses, which cause my eyes to close as I feel your bliss

Such an amazing kiss!

This taste is addicting and it's something I prefer not to miss.

Still grasping your bottom lip as I gently taste the wine off your lips

Tonight, I yield to be controlled by your kiss...

Take another sip and let me

kiss the wine off your lips.

Satori Unwrapped...

Alone In My Pantomime

Alone in the shower and got caught up in this experience within my mind

Streams of water showering as I'm "ALONE IN MY PANTOMIME"

The feel of the water captivates me as my eyes are closed lost in time

Moved by images of you have me imaginatively acting out my next moment with you

Yes, you move me and your image suspends me

Locked in this imaginative experience we caress each other as we listen to Eric Benet

So real as I move gracefully with you as we kiss while our tongues play

No rush in movement.

This pantomime is happening in the shower while my movement is silent

Locked in the movement I follow the wet stream desiring to play where the emotions are raised

I hold your body and you become supple as if you were doing ballet

This pantomime is beyond temptation!

It's an imaginative permission inviting some stimulation, allowing me to touch your intuition

I'm still swaying gracefully lost in my mind

as I'm caught up in this pantomime!

Let Me Read Your Manual

After 11pm talk with you is in order

You are entitled to be at ease baby

I just want to say you are made for love.

You are also built to be explored and experienced

Let me kiss your manual so I can follow the original design of your makeup.

Some lessons are sweet to the soul so I'm eager to learn

I hunger for your lessons

Kissing your manual equips me with knowing how you function

I desire to learn how you work.

I'm open to learning your range of motion while I strengthen your hip flexor

You say there are other ways to work you

I guess I need to memorize this manual to see how many ways to work you!

Satori Unwrapped...

My Aromatherapy

You are my aromatherapy

The scent and sense of your femininity draws me

Not a manufactured scent but the pleasant scent from your heart

Your therapeutic scent relaxes the nerve endings within mind

As a man I call this consolation.

Your scent is an innocent seduction

You don't have to say a word--your scent moves me to an erection

The power of your femininity alters my mental direction.

Your heart is likened to a lilac spring garden that gives comfort to my masculinity.

Your heart scent entices my sense of smell and speaks softly.

You are like a slow burning 30-inch incense that measures time erotically

As the time ticks the cloud of your scent fills the room

Your energy is captivating.

This is a liberating control you exercise upon me because your sensual dominance pins me with your scent-of-divinity

No doubt your scent enlarges the sensual-cloud in the room as we exchange sexually.

We share our orgasm jointly and now we are breathing each other's air

The scent of your heart made me experience your aromatherapy.

Satori Unwrapped...

Tasting Merlot

Can I taste you, Merlot?

Tasting you touches the unknown

Split glass fused together can encase you but it can't define you.

Your taste is your definition and you, my dear are called: Merlot.

The only way to embrace you...is to taste you.

Tasting you is supported by the gravity of what can come together

You are a diverse taste encased in one glass but must be experienced multi-dimensionally

All I can say is: "I love the tasting of Merlot!"

Tasting you welcomes the unknown

The taste of you has to be experienced in four different ways.

This taste has to be experienced: physically, sensually, imaginatively, and intuitively

Tasting you is best described by what you are not.

You can't be defined as Gamay

You are a variety of a unifying taste that causes my palate to play

No doubt, a sip of you in my mouth must stay.

I'm patience as I swallow you.

I hold you in my mouth as if I was holding you in a glass.

Round and plentiful

Allowing my tongue to follow your curves as if it was the hip of the glass

Such a taste that I can't pass

Your taste doesn't dwindle quickly but it lingers

Your taste remains even when I taste you off my fingers.

Your aroma of an earthy scent mixed with currant soothes me

The body of your taste is velvety, silky, and mildly sticky

I love your taste because you impressed my memory

I enjoy every moment sipping you, tasting you, and swallowing you.

Your flavor is simply

Merlot

Satori Unwrapped...

Your Music

I want to touch your music

Harmony, rhythm, notes, tunes, and sound emanates from your body.

Your inner sounds can be heard from your special acoustic

Your beauty is a melody written on your body

Your music arouses

Your music inspires

Your music excites

Your music invites--- me to explore you until I can get your inner notes to perspire.

The colors of your notes are highlighting your red chakra

Stimulated, and I can taste the sound of your acoustics

You're sending melodies that invite an intimate mantra

I can hear your music!

I can feel your music!

I can see your music!

I'm caught in a note and the only way out is to eat it.

Call this tasteful music!

Right now I hear watery acoustics

I invite your melodies on top of me

Connect with this instrument and let our sounds elevate.

This sound is silent poetry locked inside harmony

Your music is inviting me poetically

Each note allows my ideas to grow like a tree.

You are now on high and your inner rhythms oozes acoustically on my abs

I welcome your liquid lips as I'm holding your hips

Release your music.....locked into each note

Sensation is what your music promotes

Gently touching the stanzas on your body

Kissing each note as I play with your harmony

Our notes bring us close to our shared melody

As you sit upon me, we call this song...Intimacy

Damn, I love your music baby!

Satori Unwrapped...

I Crave You

I simply crave you!

This draw surpasses my nutritional needs and is yearning for another supplement

Water suffices because my body is composed of it

However, to experience an ecstasy I need your bodily ecstatic flow

We can experience this rise if we follow our sensual appetites

This craving demands bodily enclosure.

Solely wrapped up in our magnetic energy

that is fueled libidinally

by the orgasmic target we both desire.

We can compare this to fire,

but blowing it won't be enough

because we need something higher!!

No rush

You need patience?

No problem!

You say you want to be heard, I can listen to what your essence is speaking.

You need sensitivity?

No problem!

Every move will be paid attention too.

You desire to be held?

No problem!

You can be held and comforted as your pulsation activates your orgasmic flow

You desire to be heard?

No problem!

I'll create a platform so you can be heard, even if it requires standing and stretching.

You want confidentiality?

No problem!

We'll escape in the moment and I'll let you climb

I have a large appetite and I'm ready to dine!

Satori Unwrapped...

Call Me Water

Hey, you desire to get watered?

Your heart is soil and my passion is water that will help your flower to grow.

You need a description?

Call me water!!

I can take shape to match any empty crevice.

As we entertain each other, please realize it will be wet, fluid, refreshing, and soothing!

Try to go without me and see how soon you'll thirst!

You don't have to worry because you'll never thirst or be in a desert.

I'm a combination of calmness, strength, and softness--all in one!

When you need strength, I can build up pressure.

When you need calmness, the sound of my drippings will relax you.

When you need softness, I'm pliable enough to carouse you.

Call me....Water!

You can see me flow as a stream that touches every stone consistently and softly

You can see me as rain as I wet wherever I may fall.

I drip from the highest peak...to the lowest valley

I can transform from the hardest to the softest

I can change the driest condition to the wettest.

Like water....I 'm indiscriminate

I moisten and nourish everything.

I flow like the waterfall.

No will... No struggle

Just serving....just flowing.

Take the lid off your glass and watch how I will refresh you

Just call me Water!

Satori Unwrapped...

Your Enchanting Energy

Enchanted by your energy

Your essence stirs the server in me.

I have ways to utilize your own energy to relax you.

Tonight-let me serve you with different liquid solaces.

To bring a balance I'll play with the hot and cold.

Understand this energy is active and soothes you all over-including your soul!

When you need deep penetration, I'll use the liquid heat

When you need that tension relieved, I can use cold ice within my mouth

Enchanted you are.

I'll glaze your body with ice until it becomes liquid in my mouth

The liquid changes temperature as the ice melts in my mouth.

Tongue is lubricated.

Each drip taps your sensual points

As you respond I'll use the heat from my tongue to give you a heat treatment.

As you flinch, the heat from my lips massaging the lining of your frame will relax you.

This enchanting feeling is your own energy that I'm using to soothe you.

Instead of you pleasuring yourself, I'll become you and touch your body where "you" desire

All this enchanting energy is coming from you.

Your own energy is enchanting...

let me take your temperature.

Satori Unwrapped...

Traveling Water Drops

Soft kiss on the neck and a soft whisper says: "I value you"

Just a mood desiring to escape

Night is on ease with no distractions.

Got the shower turned on warm like a hot sauna.

In the shower drawing pictures on each other with the dew upon our skin

I'm slowly following the path of the water drops as they travel south.

Enraptured in the sound of the water as it touches your skin

Absorbing the feel of the water as each water drop touches your sacred area

In that moment....I follow that one, solitary drop

It travels from your hair to your cheek bone...to your lips...drips to the crevice of your chest

continuing to flow to your navel-suspended there-until it is filled,

then flows downward to your next crevice

Here this one solitary water drop gets lost

Since I'm following the drops....I guess I'm lost too.

This crevice seems to transform water drops into living streams

ready to erupt and shoot like a geyser

Still in the shower but the nozzle is now turned off

This experience ends...with me enjoying your living streams

Go ahead and spray baby!!!

Satori Unwrapped...

Something Fitting

Nothing fancy

Nothing dreamy

No drinks

No gimmicks

No rehearsed games

I'm into something that is unique, but fitting for us.

Originality is sexy and sacred in some sense

Of course we desire to be touched but tonight let's do some unique touching

Something that combines using our breath

Something that will stretch us as we unwind

Something that can relax us as a glass of wine.

Something that allows us to be open unto each other

Something that will free our minds

Something that will makes us vulnerable

Something that will make our hearts penetrable

Something that can stir us erotically

Tonight, you and I will do "partner yoga"

I desire to engage in a nice sensual stretch

Let me be your base and you be the frame

You pull and I'll push

In our calmness we whisper each other's names

You bend and I'll stretch

This night it's about flexibility

A fusion of masculinity and femininity

Sharing each other breath is an ecstasy!

The more flexible we are, the more our sacred areas can expand

Such a unique night because what is stretched shall be contracted

Fit and stretch yourself on me baby

Yes, this type of yoga makes this night a perfect fit.

Satori Unwrapped...

I'm Intrigued

I'm intrigued by your sensual stanza

Your breath activates my stamina

Your company revivifies

Your energy helps simplifies

Your touch electrifies

Your conversation edifies

Our time together will only intensify

My attention is concentrated

Highly engaged until my feelings can't be debated.

The only thing on our agenda is time.

Chemistry radiating from each other smells like sweet lime

Your gestures seems to rhyme

Our breath...Our desires...Our emotions....Our words...Our silence...and our touching makes our mood sublime.

Your initiation and erotic prowess puts me in a stasis

I'm motionless

I'm breathless

There's an openness

Our chemistry is fearless

As I caress you I can sense your tenderness

Rhythmic gyration

Intoxicating penetration

Absent of hesitation

Mood filled with flirtation

Love muscles anticipating stimulation

A time of searching

Our energy is conversing

Spontaneous flow with no room for rehearsing

Tonight, I fell prey to a new addiction.

This experience tastes like a sweet concoction.

Satori Unwrapped...

Can I Touch You?

Just wondering if I could touch you?

Can I caress you with my eyes..?

Can my presence massage your aura?

Is it ok if my voice touches your thoughts..?

Are you ok with my laughter touching your imagination?

Is it alright if my silence touches your wishes?

Can I mentally touch you before you experience my physical touch?

I'm interested in researching you before I explore you.

Trying to comfort you without any preliminary activities

Truly desire to know you, therefore I want to connect with your energy.

If you are ok with keeping the door open....is it ok to throw away the key?

No need to lock the doors, just keep it open for me.

Just curious, is it alright if I can touch you..?

Satori Unwrapped...

An Empty Canvass

If this canvass was empty

What would you paint?

My desires and ideas are plenty

The scent of your inner fire is heavenly

Drawing this picture as your temperature is rising.

Random and the mood keeps things surprising

The light on this canvass is steaming.

My tongue is the brush and your canvass is waiting

Soft strokes with my tongue is mesmerizing

Your lower energy points are connecting

This stroke of my tongue has you jumping

Your love muscle is speaking.

The tip of this brush captures your lip peaking

Your eyes are closed and this tongue has you dreaming

Yes, I'm patiently drawing.

I have your mind and yes I'm massaging

Your canvas is being filled and colored with my feelings.

I measure your frame by our anticipated pleasure

Drawing circles until your desires are hovering

Inspired by the hovering cloud my tongue continues with the drawing

This painting is abstract.

The image is clear as you contract.

Even strokes by this brush increases as I softly poke.

Now needing your input.

We need to mix some colors.

Our paint needs some water

Just enough so it remains thick

but easy enough so the stroke is slick.

A work of art.

Satori Unwrapped...

Sensational Taste

Chocolate, I love the sensation of our tongues speaking.

Spark heat...Fire

A fire that cannot be contained.

Your touch electrifies the fine hairs on the back of my neck.

Is this the tangible expression of love?

I taste you.

Your passion delights my lips.

Water flows from between my hips.

Eager for another taste of your warmth.

Don't mind me as a posture myself to receive.

Your essence.

Waste not, I dearly want each ounce.

Each ounce, each pound of you.

You wet my appetite.

You linger on my tongue.

The sensation.

The ridges.

The pleasure.

The engorgement leaves me breathless.

Insatiable.

Pleasurable

Cream, you are delightful

Ummm your taste energizes my palate.

These signal has my tongue feeling erotic.

Pulsating

I'll use my teeth to clinch your back until you increase your breathing.

Yes ma' my energy is seething

I'll capture your breath and recycle it back until your love muscles start jumping.

I'll kiss your ear until your gateway is clear

You signals only send soothing tingles

I love when you dance because I like to see your hips wiggle.

I enjoy your gyration as it activates your lubrication

I just want to drink like I was drinking libation.

Chocolate, attend your eyes to my brown skin.

Melanin has blessed these erect nipples to perfection.

Taste each one.

They hold the power of the mighty river.

Turn into me.

I am your visual entertainment.

Entrapped in the web of pleasure.

I wait on my knees for you.

You are my king.

I am yours, whole and complete.

Focus on the orifice that's at your service.

I challenge myself to embrace every inch.

To report to the base for duty.

I service you, indebted to your love.

The motion between us is seamless.

Riveting and shaking me to my core.

How can love taste this good, this sweet, and this spicy?

As your beloved Queen, anoint me from the cistern of love. Let your liquid flow from my head, across my lips, to my feet. Drown me.

Cream, this ointment is sacred

Each drip adds into to the ocean of your chasm.

A dwelling liquid solace that'll glaze your lid.

Let it pop up and squirt as I drink from your divine liquid.

Satori Unwrapped...

When Sensual & Erotica Meet

The moment when sensual and erotica meet

A moment when two energies meet.

A request for your energy to speak.

No time restraint, just two being discrete.

Sensual and erotica touching until your love energy excretes.

Anyone can penetrate, if you let them in.

However, you desire to graduate beyond just physical penetration.

That experience is moot in and of itself.

You need something pacing.

You need random moments that sends you racing.

Heighten until all you can feel is your breathing.

You are demanding something greater.

Your essence is inviting a sensual penetration

I hear your essence asking for an intellectual penetration

Nothing like a brain teaser!

You want vulnerability with no censor

Your essence needs an emotional penetration

You want a heartfelt and purposeful experience

You need someone that understands the sensual and erotica science

Let's be honest, you are needing a full sexual invasion

You are due this memorable occasion.

You need that experience that floods your heart and mind afterwards

You desire that yang that is aware when you are peaking

You want that yang that is there to capture you as you are leaking

You need an experience that'll have your body speaking

You want to be exhausted in breath until you collapse while you are folding

You want that freedom until you are no longer holding

You need that type of sex equivalent to meditation

You want that kiss, touch, and energy that becomes your medication.

Satori Unwrapped...

life

Life is a lesson. Our trials, chaos and ignorance are opportunities to learn. In our bliss, peace, and enlightenment there are also opportunities to learn. It's in our life lessons that we advance ourselves and help improve the human condition. Let us learn to embrace our life lessons.

Satori Unwrapped...

Be Encouraged

Express yourself completely...then keep quiet.

Be like the forces of nature:

when it blows, there is only wind;

when it rains, there is only rain;

when the cloud passes, the sun shines through.

Open yourself to the Tao (way of Love),

then trust your natural responses (as they are governed by love);

and everything will fall in place. — Tao Te Ching Verse 23 by Lao Tzu

This source of wisdom inspired me and sustained me as I faced one of the lowest points in life. To understand "how" things should be, births a patience to know the storms of life eventually rescind back to normalcy. Storms and tornados in life are exaggerated forces that can't occur continuously. They only occur for a short period of time. Patience works on our behalf to know that we can see pass the storms or tornados in life because these forces must forfeit to nature's state of normalcy. Why respond to storms and tornados when you know they are not designed to function daily? To venture deeper, they help re-balance us or our situations. Truth is, we need storms and tornados. They help sustain nature.

Be encouraged and be like nature!

Satori Unwrapped...

Being a Person of Value

Strive to be a person of value. People keep, embrace, attract to, and promote what they perceive as valuable. In retrospect people dismiss or reject that which they don't perceive as valuable.

Within relationships we must ask:

"What value do I bring?"

"Will my value add to your value?"

"Is our self-perceived value comparable to each other?"

If we are personally doubting our own value then we are less confident and driven to build value within our potential love-interest or to a relationship.

Relationships are a continual act of building value "within each other" and "with each other" in order to "serve others." It's imperative to see value in each other! If we see value then we must protect it so we don't lose sight each other's value. Relationally speaking, if our potential love-interest can't explain, identify, or mention how they value YOU and EACH OTHER--understand this is a sign of a future rejection or dismissal.

To prevent a future dismissal or rejection, we must invest into building value within ourselves first. After we build value within then we should to assist building value in our potential love-interest. The goal is to reciprocate building value in one another. If we perceive ourselves as being valuable, we generate a "cause-of-energy" that will build the "effect" of a valuable relationship.

When two people see value in something, they are more inclined to fight for and protect what they value. When one fails to see value, it leaves only one fighting for what they value. In maturity, we must seek interest in someone that views US as valuable. If they see value in you--they will fight with you, for you, and will strive to protect you.

This type of value is something a relationship will not dismiss.

Satori Unwrapped...

Listening To Love Speak

Desire to be fluent in each other's love languages because relationships revolves around the language of love.

– Gerald "Satori" Seals

Every heart has an ability to be loved and to share love. Our hearts can be reached as we learn the languages that speak love to our hearts. If we all have a love language then that means love speaks. To learn each other's language is to learn each other methods of communicating love. Relationships are stimulated by communication. It's through communication that our relationships become stronger.

If we look at the word communication the prefix commun- means 'to share'. To venture further, the prefix commun- is directly related to the word 'commune' which is the root word in 'Community'. The word commune is equivalent to the Latin word "communio' which means to wall together and to fortify.

Communication allows our relationships to become stronger if we are continually sharing information to and about each other. Likewise, a relationship will be breached if two fail to share information to and about each other. Knowing each other's love languages brings a sense of community to one another. This sense of community is strengthened according to shared information or knowledge. Having a sense of community also brings a spiritual, mental, and moral strength to one another, which increases the sense of endurance. A relationship that doesn't bring a sense of community is a relationship that will rob our spiritual, mental, and moral strength, in turn lessening our sense-of-endurance.

We each express our love languages differently. Some of the ways we express love are known through:

1. Verbal expression – expresses love through the spoken and written word. Also through verbal compliments.

2. Serving – show love by doing things or showing acts of kindness.

3. Creating opportunities – show love by trying to inspire someone into their greater self. One who looks for ways to open opportunities for the person they love.

4. Touch – expresses love by physically touching, such as hugs and kisses.

5. Time – expresses love by the time they share with someone. Therefore, they enjoy doing things together with their love interest.

6. Gifts – expresses love by giving random gifts, cards. Etc. **Book: The Five Love Languages by Gary Chapman**

Therefore, in order to relate we must properly hear each other's languages of love. To say we're in a relationship whether it's platonic, social, romantic, and/or erotic means admitting: YOU ARE SPEAKING MY LANGUAGE. Our relational problems are LANGUAGE BARRIERS. We remove barriers by LEARNING EACH OTHER LANGUAGES. Relationships are a path to unity. Language is the bridge to UNITY. To rediscover unity in our relationships is to discover each other love languages. To solve relational conflicts or problems is to listen to what LOVE is saying. We must ask ourselves what are we listening too!

Satori Unwrapped...

Relationships Fail but We Are Not Defected

A relationship ought to be a continual process of bringing value to each other. – Gerald "Satori" Seals

A relationship should add worth to us spiritually, mentally, domestically, socially, and financially. Anything that doesn't add worth isn't worth investing into. Relationships are value-added and are not an arrangement of defection. If we may be transparent, when we experience a divorce or break-up from a meaningful relationship our hearts may feel "defected."

Everyone is different, but there's a period when the heart feels incapacitated spiritually, mentally, and socially after a divorce or break-up. This inner deprived feeling comes from the relationship losing its value or has shifted in value. For visual understanding, when a product is produced and it comes out faulty the press operator will mark that product as a "DEFECT." Once marked, Quality Control throws the product away or disposes of it.

This is how many people feel after a relationship has failed. We feel DEFECTED and thrown away. Having this feeling is what we call a heart-break, which is actually the feeling of DEFECTION. Sadly, many people close themselves off prevent having this experience again. In the process we often fail to discover why or how we feel defected.

DEFECTION is felt when the value has been compromised, which creates a deficiency. In other words, a defected feeling follows when we have a relation void. To reverse this feeling is to rebuild value within ourselves. The first step in building value is to value ourselves. To value ourselves is to love ourselves. From here, everything will eventually re-align itself around activities, relationships, or energies that will restore value back within us.

To move pass experiencing future defections within our relationships, we must realize:

1. Relationships should add peace and not confusion
2. Relationships should recycle love and forgiveness and not hate and resentments
3. Relationships should boost our esteem and not lower it
4. Relationships should primarily encourage and not discourage us
5. Relationships should validate and not hinder us
6. Relationships should bring a freedom without feeling stifled

LESSON: Break-ups happen but we don't have to stay DEFECTED.

Satori Unwrapped...

We Are Intimate...Therefore I See You

Intimacy is an ability to see you in me and I in you. — Gerald "Satori" Seals

True intimacy removes the duality existing between two. In pure intimacy, a relationship is about oneness/unity and not duality. This subtly points reveals that intimacy is shared or experienced as two practice removing their ego from dominating their relationship. The insertion of ego can shift the attitude in a relationship to measuring each other according to what we can solely gain selfishly from our love interest. This subtle attitude will cause a relationship to be "performance based" and not "service based." Bear in mind, in essence a relationship is about serving each other. To do the opposite is to have a relationship based upon serving each other's self-interests. Ultimately this erodes intimacy.

Erosion is experienced because serving one another shifts into controlling or assisting some type of self-serving agenda. To prevent erosion of intimacy, we must practice thinking beyond ourselves. To achieve this means to:

1. See beyond our own interests
2. Be open to one another's opinions and views
3. Be able to self-correct and see/understand ourselves
4. Develop an ability to see through one another's eyes

Ego can be defined as being overly interested or consumed with our own personal interests until love and forgiveness no longer motivate our decisions. The removal of self-agendas convert duality into unity. Union is created because two people no longer see themselves as two but as one. This union can be described as self-forgetfulness, which creates solace for one another.

A true union is two people seeing themselves IN each other. A wisdom source to reference is Genesis 3:25: "and they were both naked, the man and woman, and were not ashamed." This scripture highlights intimacy. The Hebrew/Aramaic word for "naked" is arah (aw-raw). Arah refers to 'pouring out or emptying'. Inferring into this word clarifies that intimacy is an ongoing process of getting empty from our self-agendas and egos. The Hebrew/Aramaic word for "ashamed" is kalam (kaw-lawm). Kalam defines "ashamed" as: taunting or insulting. According to the definition of ashamed, intimacy is prevented when our relationship avoid:

1) Tempting one another into an offense or anger
2) Challenging one another in a mocking way
3) Highlighting each other imperfections with the intent to bring condemnation
4) Using overbearing speech to incite bitter feelings

Satori Unwrapped...

Another place to recognize intimacy is Genesis 3:23, which reads: "Adam said, this is now bone of my bone and flesh of my flesh." According to Adam's declaration, we recognize intimacy involves being able to "see" into each other. This joint-penetrant insight brings two into a place of BEING and BECOMING.

Intimacy is measured by seeing how two people can see themselves inside each other. Embracing this as a source of measurement provides additional insight: Intimacy is increased or decreased based upon the level two people are able to jointly see within each other. Evidence of this joint-sight is revealed in our:

1.) Heart-fusion (unity)

2.) Sacredness within our relationship

3.) Joint-penetrant insight into one another

4.) Ability to not judge one another

5.) Joint-mental stimulation

6.) Ability to exude joint-trust

Intimacy can also be explained as joint-expression. This defines the effects of two penetrating each other's soul. Intimacy takes two self-expressions and gradually removes the "self" until two see themselves inside one another. Truly, this is when two become one and this is true intimacy. We know we are intimate when we can look at our love interest and say: I SEE YOU!

Satori Unwrapped...

Love Didn't Hurt Us

The greatest thing we can do is rise above our hurts and still choose to love. – Gerald "Satori" Seals

It is important to understand there exists no "ill will" within love. Our hurts comes from aspects of self-will. Love simply is! Some of us who have read scripture or other wisdom texts will notice when LOVE is talked about it is descriptive, active, and presented as an existence. The dilemma is our hearts are directed by our wills (desire) and must yield to the true existence of Love. When a heart is not yielded to love, hurt and negative outcomes shall follow.

We have allowed others who have misrepresented love to blur our view into thinking it was love that hurt us. Today, understand love didn't hurt us. The hurt came from someone operating against the ways of love and the results of these actions have caused hurt, disappointment and/or pain. This is why forgiveness is highly needed because it re-aligns our hearts into love when our hearts has been displaced. We all have been hurt and will continue to experience hurt as we continue to live.

The higher degree of love allows us to absorb the hurt and to ascend above the pain. This may appear foreign because we are taught to harbor our hurt and put up shields. To go deeper, love brings transparency within ourselves. True love is not driven by SELF (ego) the less of SELF (ego) the less we'll get hurt. This is why we shouldn't fear love because to fear it give rise to SELF (ego). If we become transparent, we will discover we continue to hurt and hold on to the memories because part of the SELF (ego) has been momentarily detached from love.

There's power in love. Take down the walls and use love as our shield and we will soon discover we will hurt less. Why, because we no longer love with the intention of everything revolving around "Self (ego)" thereby we become love and that is all we will desire to do. As we grow in love, we will project love, in addition to having power to rise above our hurt.

Satori Unwrapped...

Our Desire to Connect With Someone

There's a dynamic for every relationship. Therefore, we choose the dynamic that we desire to relate with. – Gerald "Satori" Seals

Desiring to connect with someone is a natural desire. We are social beings, which implies we all will have the desire to connect with someone. Truly, the purpose to connect with another person is to help bring out their beauty. In pure intention, relationships should bring out our beauty.

However, we don't see beauty in some relationships because of a connection issue. These connection issues comes from not practicing the "principle of connection." The "principle of connection" teaches that, we can't connect with others if we're not connected within ourselves. Finding our own connection with ourselves is the gateway to connecting with others.

In our quest for connection we must ask two questions. First, we should ask if we are connected to ourselves; and, second, we should ask if we bring an energy and spirit that someone desires to connect with.

Go Into a Relationship with What You Desire To Leave With

If we go in desiring harmony, we can go out in peace even if the relationship takes another direction. – Gerald "Satori" Seals

Truth is: some relationships exhaust themselves. The question we must ask ourselves is: Can we handle it when the exhaustion happens? How will be respond when someone's heart shifts into another direction? Am I mature enough to remain a friend despite we were once intimate in each other?

Sadly, the response to exhaustion creates havoc or potentially brings ruin to relationships. When we focus on bringing good to each other, knowing the relationship could potentially exhaust itself, it leaves room to take away the good aspects of the relationship and releasing the bad. An unanticipated result from an exhausted relationship entered into with this mindset would be peace and the ability to see good in each other, despite the ending.

Satori Unwrapped...

Rising Above Gender Vices

In true essence, man and woman are not designed to dominate each other but to complement each other.

— Gerald "Satori" Seals

Celebrating and complaining about gender vices will extend gender strife. In true essence, man and woman are not to be at war or odds with each other. Truthfully, we have created barriers that produce strife and conflicts. To rectify this clash of opinions we must learn how the female and male energies truly complement each other. To learn, we need iterations of knowledge and understanding about both energies. As lessons are learnt, we can effectively serve each other. We need to learn:

1.) How each gender thinks

2.) How each gender responds to issues

3.) How each genders' emotions are driven

4.) The differences between the genders

The foundation to all relationships is not solely love!!! The foundation to relationships also requires knowledge and understanding each other. Meaning: love is operative, which keeps the relationship vibrant, functional and full of life. Love without a knowledge and understanding will challenge the love that two people have for each other. Think about it: the more we know and understand each other, the more we can love each other. Healthy relationships are experienced among those that have spent time learning to know and understand each other thoroughly.

Satori Unwrapped...

Love Doesn't Produce Confusion

Confusion can't be found within a loving heart. – Gerald "Satori" Seals

Love doesn't create or produce confusion. We have to ask the question: Why do we see so much confusion in life? Answer: the more we remove our hearts from love the more we allow room for confusion. There's a process that removes our hearts from love and the result of this process is: confusion.

The first process of removal occurs when we're separated from practicing love and when we refuse to learn the practices of love. Secondly, the process of removal occurs when we fail to practice seeing love within ourselves. Thirdly, the process of removal occurs when we fail to practice seeing love in other people. Peace and confusion begins with us and is contained within our hearts. Therefore, peace and confusion exists because the heart projects it into life. Confusion comes from a confused heart. Peace comes from a peaceful heart.

We witness confusion because an individual or people have rejected the practices of love, only see confusion within themselves, and only can respond or attract to the confusion in others. A passage within the Book of Life (Bible) states, "LET THERE BE LIGHT." This statement was targeted at darkness (confusion). To deal with confusion requires intelligence. Intelligence is needed in order to bring peace to confusion. We need an intelligence that will encourage ourselves and others to practice love, develop our ability to see love within ourselves, and develop our ability to see love in others.

LESSON: Confront confusion with intelligence.

Satori Unwrapped...

Quantum Attractions

"From every human being there rises a light that reaches straight to heaven, and when two souls that are destined to be together find each other, the streams of light flow together and a single brighter light goes forth from that united being."

~Ba'al Shem Tov

Relationships are based upon "Quantum Attractions." In other words, it is about the dynamic and not the romantic phenomena first. Relationships are attraction. Therefore, relationships revolves around energy. When two become one they are actually compressing energy to the point that it elevates to a higher frequency. The source of attraction is the heart. Meaning, the base of our attraction draws the energy from the conscience, will, libido, motive, intention, mindset, and spirit. Truly this is the true essence of a person--their HEART.

To primarily relate based on charisma, preferences, or some preconceived image, will delude us from seeing the heart, which is the source of attraction. When two are single in heart, they can find their "heart-mate." Why, because the frequency of their heart will pull them together— ATTRACTION. The confirmation of this discovery will be witnessed as each heart feels elevated to a higher pitch or frequency (high level of excitement and joy). The higher frequency becomes soothing to both hearts to the point it attracts them to become one. This true oneness, an elevation of heart (frequency), is the elevated state our hearts are attracted too.

The desire for a relationship is really our heart desiring to change its' frequency to a more elevated state. Sadly, some of our relationships do the opposite. We are doing the opposite because some of us don't focus on attracting the heart of a person. We are designed to fall in love with the heart and not with preferences or other deluding facades. Becoming one, is a reward for the heart to experience an elevation or to have access to a higher frequency (LOVE).
Relationships are to be beautiful--ATTRACT ACCORDINGLY.

Satori Unwrapped...

Love Is Visible

Love is like fresh water that cleanses the heart, which enables the eyes to see love in life. – Gerald "Satori" Seals

Coming into an awareness to see love in ourselves is the gateway to see love in others. To say we don't see love in our lives is to say we don't see love in ourselves. Within our being is love because our original self-image is love. Life challenges, experiences, and a variety of social occurrences causes our "image of love" to become cloaked by dense images such as jealousy, strife, and conceit. The result of these dense images will cause hearts to become removed from love.

Our hearts influence what we see in life. A heart of love will see love in life and a heart of jealousy will see life as a competition. If we bend our hearts to love we'll realize love is present everywhere. Therefore, we must ask ourselves the question: What do we see when we look at ourselves? Areas where love is absent simply means love is hiding behind an individuals' ability to see it within themselves.

We Are Beautiful

Beauty is evident to those that see beauty within themselves. – Gerald "Satori" Seals

Beauty is being able to embrace our flaws without feeling inferior to others. They say: "beauty is in the eye of the beholder." Beauty is something that exalts, heightens, or moves our senses, mind, and spirit. This is why beauty remains in the eyes of the beholder because different things exalts, heightens, and moves us, individually. Our eyes and hearts behold beauty, so this means we bring beauty to each other in life.

Seeing the beauty in ourselves, despite our flaws, allows beauty to be identifiable. Beauty is measured not by admiration or looks but according to our ability to inspire or impress others. For example, if a unanimous group says something is beautiful they're measuring how they were impressed by beauty. This means beauty doesn't exists solely for itself rather beauty has the ability to influence. To say something is beautiful is to say we were influenced by an attraction that elevated our awareness in appreciation of the attraction.

True beauty doesn't demand attention but it inspires. Meaning, people that are considered beautiful are inspiring and not egotistical. Today, practice seeing beauty within ourselves so we can inspire others into beauty. People that are inspiring or bring inspiration to others are the true definition of being beautiful. We all can inspire, therefore we are beautiful. As we inspire more and see beauty within ourselves the more people will measure "US" as beautiful.

Satori Unwrapped...

A Good Relationship Begins With You

A good relationship begins with you being what you desire.—Gerald "Satori" Seals

If we want love then we must "BE" love. The one thing we can control in our relationships--is ourselves. Before we can trust someone else we must be able to trust ourselves. The source of a good relationship resides within us and we project what is within us to our boo, love interest, brown suga, queen amena, vanilla bean, carmel delight, mixed rice, or however we classify the one we desire to relate to. The Most High created us to be relational beings, therefore finding interest in one another is natural and beautiful. The base to any productive and flourishing relationship is LOVE.

Begin with love and stay with love and it won't steer you wrong. If your relationship is suffering a little turbulence, take a pause-for-the-cause and refocus on our base, LOVE. A good relationship is able to replenish each other with love, forgiveness and simplicity. One of the most beautiful things in life, is two people truly into each other. The more we celebrate love, the more we will see others willing to share love with us, for like-minded people shall attract each other. Meaning: a person of love shall attract another person of love.

LESSON: If we desire a good relationship we must make ourselves available to love and everything else will take care of itself.

Satori Unwrapped...

Pair Forgiveness with Your History

Self-forgiveness allows you to keep your past history in the past. — Gerald "Satori" Seals

We all have a history, what we are today will soon be tomorrow. Therefore, today is your history. During our life course, we will experience moments where events or people will try or strive to stain your history. How we respond to it also becomes part of our history.

Be advised, forgive those who strive to stain your history. If you think about it in "practice" your history will be paired with forgiveness and not un-forgiveness. Forgiveness contains a silent course to bring people and our awareness to truth. Un-forgiveness contains a silent course to bring people or our awareness to distortions.

A descriptive term for forgiveness is "release." As people study your history, they'll see your imperfections and realize your first truth. That first truth is that you have fallen short and will continue to fall short. Falling short is also known as being a sinner. Many people exercise power over others because they hold people in hostage about discovering a central truth about ourselves, which is we all sin and will sin (fall short) again. To pair forgiveness with your history means you become "released" from a past that others may try to keep current. When you have forgiven yourself and your past it exposes your accusers.

Accusations can only hold those in hostage who haven't been "released" from their past. When you forgive your history you become released (from a spiritual or psychological prison) to move forward into your future. Those that feed on your past shortcomings will soon discover the history of your forgiveness has released you from living in your past. As your accusers continue to search your history and your ability to forgive, they will realize the truth: They are the only one living in your past.

INSIGHT: Un-forgiveness makes your history a static record. Forgiveness makes your history a living record. Having a living record means you can always change your history. Forgiving our errors today is forgiving our yesterday, which is history. A forgiven history releases you to continue to write your history. After a while, people that reads your history will realize you were just living.

Satori Unwrapped...

Spend Time to Learn Our Mates Thoughts

It's important to understand our love-interest or mate THOUGHT LIFE. The result of our relationships will display in each person's THOUGHTS towards each other and life. It's advisable to KNOW the THOUGHTS of our mate. If you want to see the FUTURE in our relationships learn of each other thoughts.

INSIGHT: We can predict the future within our relationships by understanding our mate or potential mate thought life.

MORAL: Investing into our mate thought life is investing into the future of our relationship.

We are the Source to Solve Our Problems

Because of our indifference of heart we closet ourselves from our own truth, solutions, and answers. Our needed truth, solution, and answer for the most part will be indifferent from our current state of reality or heart.

To accept our needed truth, solution, and answer requires us to open our heart and mind to what is different from what we perceive. Once this becomes a practice we will find ourselves solving many of our own problems. As we solve our own problems we can then graduate to solve others' problems.

INSIGHT: As I solve my problems I can also solve my brotha's, sista's and humanity problems

Satori Unwrapped...

The Secret to Finding Our Mate

When one stops seeking for a mate one will become open to FIND their mate. --Gerald "Satori" Seals

Seeking implies striving to discover something that matches our preferences, bias, emotional leanings, wants (instead of needs), etc. To seek also implies someone is to be in pursuit! Expecting to be pursued is actually "demanding" to be overtook or captured. Being overtook or captured also reveals a desire to be chased or to possess a "chase-me-mentality."

Embodying a "chase-me-mentality" causes the pure desire for a relationship to becoming a "game." Gamesmanship is evident because as one captures what they've pursued, they feel like they won a prize. If we are honest, this type of thinking dominates most of our psyches. To push this understanding further the "chase-me-mentality" or the "desire to be pursued" serves as the cause for the effects of GAMESMANSHIP. The games men and women play can be connected to the "chase-me-mentality."

Due to a "chase-me-mentality", men and women entertain or adopts ways to "win" each other through stratagem, force, or guile. Desiring a relationship is not an aim to be "won" but an aim to become "connected." To become connected points to desiring to be enjoined with someone.

Embodying a "connecting-mentality" serves as the cause for the effect of "RAPPORT BUILDING." Rapport building is the result that brings two together under the "connecting-mentality." To add, rapport building is the tool for discovering a mate. Finding implies striving to discover someone by RECOGNIZING what their heart needs.

To recognize is to acknowledge something. The source of acknowledgement is our heart. Our potential mate is connected to our ability to acknowledge what our heart needs. Finding is a cosmic draw that brings two hearts together. Basically, heart-mates attracts to each other. Heart-mates can be synonymous with the term twin flame. This means, finding our mates is discovering what our heart needs.

The way of SEEKING or PURSUING a mate is the path towards GAMESMANSHIP. The way of FINDING or RECOGNIZING a mate is the path towards SELF-REALIZATION and RAPPORT BUILDING. To find a mate is to practice self-realization. This implies the more we become real and transparent with ourselves the easier it is to SEE or RECOGNIZE our potential mate.

Satori Unwrapped...

INSIGHT: SEEKING creates looking that prevents SEEING; PURSUING creates seeking that prevents FINDING. FINDING is the opening that recognizes our heart desires in another. RECOGNIZING our heart desires in another is the true enjoining with our HEART MATE (aka Twin Flame).

Satori Unwrapped...

Learning Tolerance in Order to Forgive

One key lesson of forgiveness is tolerance. – Gerald "Satori" Seals

We cannot learn forgiveness until we learn tolerance. Becoming less responsive to offenses is tolerance. Lessening our responsiveness to offenses occurs when we practice sympathy or compassion for different beliefs, practices, or acts differing or conflicting with our own perspective. Hearts that are able to show tolerance are forgiving hearts. The very nature of tolerance enables us to see past or overlook an offense in order to achieve reconciliation. The ingredient of forgiveness brings about our inward freedom and growth. Without forgiveness, spiritual growth will be hindered. We are able to move past the imprisonment of our un-forgiveness as we practice tolerance.

INSIGHT: Learning the lessons of tolerance are lessons that lead to freedom.

Believe in Yourself

Believing in yourself empowers you to see past your own perceived limitations.—Gerald "Satori" Seals

It's desirous to have others to believe in you. However, if you believe in yourself, that is empowerment. Depending upon others to believe in you means you have given the other person power over your motivation. Being able to maintain a belief in yourself enables you to stay motivated because you have the power.

Oftentimes, pursuing a dream or vision requires you to rise up in the midst of people who don't believe in you. This is where believing in yourself benefits you because it strengthens your own power. To have power is to have influence. When you believe in yourself, you have the power to draw people that will believe in you. You have the ability to rise if you maintain believing in yourself on a consistent basis.

INSIGHT: If you believe in yourself long enough, you will eventually be surrounded by those who believe in you too.

Satori Unwrapped...

Confession of Men

Men Want Their Heart Protected

The treasure of a man is his heart, therefore he desires a partner that can protect it. — Gerald "Satori" Seals

Men innately desire a woman that naturally protects his heart. One thing men understand and sense is "protection." His silent and audible language is protection. A man will continue to roam and search until he feels assured that his heart can be protected. This points to a man's innate emotional desire that he seeks after. Men seek and desire to:

1.) Cover a woman as she covers his heart

2.) Have a woman that will defend his name and honor

3.) Have a woman that will protect his secrets

4.) Have a woman that will be a watch-woman over his heart

5.) Have a woman that can speak life into him

6.) Have a woman that creates an environment of rest and peace

7.) Have a woman that will reduce things competing for his emotions

Understand, men silently cry!! There are several things men silently cry about. One of the cries are: "Who is willing to protect my heart?" One of the reasons we see men being nomads is because we are scarred or apprehensive to lay our hearts down. Just as women, men have fears and concerns. A man will not take a relationship to another level if he can't "SEE" or "SENSE" that his heart is being protected. In the midst of being a Protector, men wonder who is going to protect the most vulnerable part of him while in life battles?

Satori Unwrapped...

Confession of Men

Ladies, Men Want You to Believe In Him

Men are motivated to build and love if he senses the woman believes in him. — Gerald "Satori" Seals

One of the sexiest things that a woman can do for a man is to believe in him. Ladies, this moves a man's heart. The non-mentioned struggle men deal with is feeling isolated in life. Men are geared to execute and build. Man remains inert if he doesn't have someone to execute and build for. It is not in man to be selfish or to be strictly into himself. Man is designed to work towards something and for others.

Ladies, your belief in man is the validation needed for him to perform. Understand, men are deliberate on how they use their energy. Believing in man is a love language that tells a man [us] that you are willing to be a partner. If a man doesn't sense that you believe in him he will rescind his drive to execute. A man will not build something if he feels that it is not valued. Men are wired to build for you. This is why he tries to solve problems by trying to do something for you (builder).

Ladies, believing in him tells him that you value him. Understand this speaks to a man's emotional need. One of man's silent cries is he wants you to believe in him. Strip the notion that a man wants his ego stroked. A man wants his heart stroked by you believing in him. Emotionally, a man feels isolated from you if you don't believe in him. This will drive the man to be "nomadic" until he no longer feels isolated from a woman.

The Book of Life describes a woman as a "consoler." Ladies, this means your energy possesses an ability to alleviate burdens or bring an ease to man. If he is battling isolation, you believing in him "consoles" him emotionally. Your belief in his abilities "eases" man [us] emotionally. The reason for this is because man's sense-of-isolation transforms into a sense-of-acceptance. This sense keeps a man from being "nomadic" because he has a consoler that believes in him. Ladies, resign from trying to stroke a man's ego, instead, believe in the man. Remember, a man desires for his heart to be stroked. You have the man once you have his heart--not his ego. Men that prefer gamesmanship need their egos stroked but not a Man-of-Purpose. Stroking his ego doesn't build him but stroking his heart will!

Satori Unwrapped...

Confession of Men

What Causes a Man to Say You're Sexy?

Sexiness is the inner radiance that emanates from the soul and speaks holistically loud from one's essence

— Gerald "Satori" Seals

What causes a man to say you're sexy? When we say you're sexy, ladies it's a compliment because we can see your state of mind or sense of self. For us to say you are sexy means we can feel and sense that your heart is finely tuned. We say, Sexy, when we hear you speak with undertones of self-love. You are considered Sexy when we can see your inner glow.

Men say Sexy when your beauty isn't defined by others but simply by you. Sexy is recognized when we can see divinity within your soul. Sexy is when your presence brings a sense of peace, stability, and growth. We say Sexy because we can feel your love as you care for others.

You are considered Sexy ladies, when we can SEE LIFE IN YOU. For a man to say you are Sexy is saying he RECOGNIZES LIFE. Why, because you are the mother-of-life! Ladies, a secret to a man's heart is to SHOW HIM THE LIFE THAT EXISTS IN YOU! Real men are attracted to the life within you! Again, we are not talking about Billy, Tyrone, or Steve but we are talking about real men with a heart that values life.

Satori Unwrapped...

Confession of Men

Ladies, Can We Build?

A man's fears are reduced when he can perceive himself building jointly with the woman. — Gerald "Satori" Seals

Men are carrying a silent desire. This desire is expressed within his question: Can we build? Ladies often wonder why it is hard for men to share our vulnerable side with you. The simple answer is FEAR. Men are innately driven to build and follow vision. Our fears comes from the potential of a woman destroying a work and vision. Hiding deep within the heart of men is the need to protect our works and vision. Remember ladies, men are protectors!

Men that are aware of their purpose are seeking and are open to women that can help advance, grow, assist, and protect the vision of our heart. By no means does this mean for a woman to forfeit her life mission. It's about enjoining and adding value to each other. Men without a legacy aren't able to reach our children's, children. As men we are effective when we can rise outside ourselves and are able to build something bigger than ourselves, which continues to speak after we are gone from this earthly plane.

As men, we desire our women to hear our hearts desires and ambitions. Ladies, if men sense that we can't lay our heads down in your laps you will never hear our vulnerable side. Men do desire to share secrets but we don't desire for our secrets to be used against us or shot back at us when a conflict arises. If this happens, men will shut down because "emotionally" we will feel like you can kill our works and vision. As men, we need touched, we crave it! Not just sexually, but we want our hearts to be touched. A woman touching a man's heart is a woman motivating a man's ability to build.

Ladies, men do not desire to be at war with you. As men, we desire to build with you. Our question is...Can we build?

Satori Unwrapped...

Confession of Men

Can Your Independence Become Interdependent

Men that are "purpose-oriented" or "clear-thinking" don't have an issue with an independent woman. Truth be told, we actually desire it. Despite popular belief or drawing from past experiences, the real problem isn't independence. If a man states a woman is too independent it doesn't mean he is negating her ability to be self-reliant. That quality is actually valued. There appears to be a trending belief that men don't value independent woman. For clarity, when a man says a woman is too independent, he is actually saying she lacks the ability to be "INTERDEPENDENT."

The conflict many face really isn't about "INDEPENDENCE" but is about "INTERDEPENDENCE." Men will say you are too independent because in perception he logically senses the woman is not inclined to partner. Within a man's mind, partnering is bringing each other's independence together to create something, which is "MUTUAL." This innate view answers his question, "Can we build together?" Men are visual, therefore if he doesn't see an ability within the woman to be "INTERDEPENDENT", this will cause him to reserve his desire to build. He will categorize the interaction according to how he views the woman.

An independent woman and man must ask themselves can they become "INTERDEPENDENT." If not, then within either gender independence will be viewed as a problem. The inability to become "INTERDEPENDENT" means there's too much of self/ego and not enough selflessness. Each gender's ability to act selfless determines the degree of their "INTERDEPENDENCE." Both genders must ask ourselves: Can we become "INTERDEPENDENT?"

Satori Unwrapped...

Confession of Men

Why Men Cheat

Men cheat because it's a resistance born of fear-- Gerald "Satori" Seals

The more a man is alone he is more inclined to wander or be nomadic. Why, because he innately desires to share himself. In his wandering and nomadic state he is looking for solace, a woman to help connect him with his emotions and vulnerabilities, feeling wanted, needing consolation, desiring assistance or help, and a sense of rest. If a man doesn't sense this, he actually feels alone, which can drive him to cheat, because he is searching.

When man is alone he is inside himself. This causes him to focus solely upon himself. This invites his spiritual nature to submit to his ego, instincts, and desires. Within ego, man views sex as:

1.) A conquest or hunt
2.) An inner competition or a game
3.) Recreation
4.) A moment of escape
5.) Control
6.) A source of identity
7.) Sense of dominance
8.) Means of pleasure
9.) Moment of excitement
10.) An opportunity to stroke an egotistical need (feeling important)
11.) Fanciful entertainment

Within ego and being alone man only see as far as his own interests. He can only see within his own emotions. He thinks only about himself. He only thinks about entertaining himself. He primarily feels or senses things if it affects him personally. An interesting thing is: a man's sexual nature is driven to SHARE. Therefore, the sexual nature in man is strong because it's a way for him to SHARE. This drive to share can be twisted in the wrong manner, which results in cheating.

Sex is also a way for a man to get outside himself. Man is built to share and give and not to be selfish. However, man's intentions becomes blurred sexually if he is unaware of himself in an alone state. Being alone puts pressure on him to be selfish, which twists his drive to share. Therefore, in an alone state he constantly entertains inner battles or conflicts. We

Satori Unwrapped...

are actually rebelling against our ego, so we share ourselves sexually in an effort to escape the torment of selfishness.

Within ourselves we wrestle with selfishness because we desire:

1.) To think about others

2.) To share our emotions

3.) To share our interests

4.) To feel like we are entertaining someone

A man absent of these four desires or being alone looks towards sexual proclivity to satisfy what we lack within ourselves. It can be said: we seek to use sex to fill our emotional, sexual, social, sensual, intellectual, and spiritual voids. Within the nature of a man we can satisfy a variety of sensations and intrapersonal needs in one sexual experience. In sex, man can feel like we are outside ourselves. Meaning, as a man has sex this may be the only time we can feel like:

1.) We are sharing

2.) We are able to feel and sense outside ourselves

3.) We are able to think outside ourselves

4.) We are entertaining (this explains why most men are concerned with performance)

When men are alone, one of the battles we must overcome is compromising our values, standards, and vision. Many overlook the fact that men desire touch. We express and communicate through touch. In a lot of ways, it shows in our sexual behavior. In pure intent we crave that touch. When we don't have it, our nomadic and wandering ways kick in.

The touch we truly crave is an all-encompassing consolation mixed with desiring an emotional, intellectual, egotistical, spiritual, social, and sensual touch. If a man doesn't sense this, we are back to being nomads as we entertain different sexual engagements. Or, the reverse happens: the man changes our interactions by becoming single and establishing platonic friendships with women. Yes there are men that get to the point of not only desiring to just have sex ladies! Not saying we won't think of it, but if we do, we will categorize the relationship so lines still exist.

Human touch is a strong need. Sadly, most men are not in touch with ourselves emotionally, sensually, and spiritually enough to explain this as a need. We do show it though. This is why we do silly things for sex or misbehave per se. In confession, many of us are guilty or has been guilty of shifting our mentality when a woman withdraws or comes up short in the touch area. This proves sex alone isn't the only touched needed. We need that conversational, emotional, mental,

Satori Unwrapped...

social, and sexual touch—all in one package. That package contains different standards for different men but at the base we need that definitive touch.

To be absent from touch for long periods of time shifts the nature of a man to become a wanderer or a nomad. He is wandering to find that all- encompassing consolation. Varying in each man's perception we see voids within ourselves. If we don't see the void being filled, we search to fill it. So, what we do is see pieces here and pieces there. If we entertain those pieces the result is we have multiple women, which includes cheating. Why, because we are looking for that full package. If it's not there, we compromise for the pieces we presently see or have access to.

In an alone state, it's important for man to reconnect with ourselves spiritually. Connecting spiritually is to kill our ego by focusing on serving, giving, loving, charity, and extending compassion. As this is done, it can change or redefine our sexual needs and views. Our orientation can shift to viewing sex as:

1.) A shared journey or joint-exploration
2.) An act of serving each other
3.) A celebration of unity
4.) A sense of being lost in each other
5.) A sense of freedom
6.) Moments of feeling high levels of selflessness
7.) Sense of vulnerability
8.) Shared spontaneity
9.) A sense of meditation because it's a form of forgetfulness
10.) A shared sacredness
11.) A shared ecstasy

As the orientation shifts to this plane of thought, man will desire intimacy and desires to be more relational with someone who shares in his magnetism. Therefore, man's wanderings becomes a purposeful search that matches his new internal orientation. Due to this changed or redefined orientation, man's tendency to cheat lessens because now sex has a purpose and meaning. Basically, he will become more mindful of who he shares himself with.

Satori Unwrapped...

Repressing our sexual desires can present a fear because now an inner conflict exists. In our alone state, we have to resist sexual urges, which become a resistance born of a fear. Sexual misbehavior can be traced to resistance, not our sexual urges. This means resistance is mental! Our urges drive us because we are resisting our "ALONENESS." Mentally, this is man's fight within ourselves if we feel we are alone. Ladies, our cheating is a resistance born of fear. This fear is BEING ALONE!

Satori Unwrapped...

About the Author

Gerald "Satori" Seals II is a leader, poet, spiritual teacher, business administrator, metaphysician, philosopher of metaphysics, and communal activist. He is known for his spiritual wisdom for everyday issues, in-depth thinking, insight, teachings, and faith. His perspectives are clearly spiritually-based, which cut across religious, political, cultural, and ethnic lines. Satori is definitely a rising spiritual thinker for the next generation. His works has availed himself for speaking engagements at faith-based organizations, churches, college groups, community groups and grass root undertakings such as the Ruwach Communal Coalition (RCC). Satori has embraced the call toward maximizing human potential, empowerment, transformation, and community.

Author Contact

Website: www.satoriseals.com
E-mail: satorigeraldseals@facebook.com
E-mail: satoriseals@gmail.com

Satori Gerald Seals

@SatoriSeals

Satori Unwrapped...

Books by Gerald "Satori" Seals:

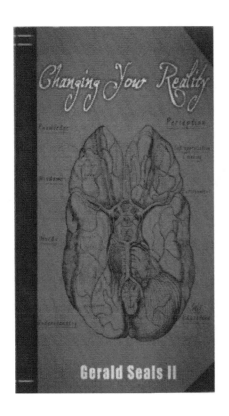

Satori Unwrapped...

Gerald Satori Seals

Developing Your Life With Wisdom

Satori Unwrapped...

Made in the USA
San Bernardino, CA
26 July 2019